HEAL ING

AN INMATE JOURNAL

THE WOUNDED HEART

Trauma Healing Institute

Facilitator's Guide

HEALING THE WOUNDED HEART: AN INMATE JOURNAL
SECOND PRINTING

© 2018 American Bible Society

ISBN 978-1-58516-127-0-a
ABS Item 124735

Adapted by Dana Ergenbright and Joy Stevens
from *Healing the Wounds of Trauma*
© 2009, 2013, 2016 Harriet Hill, Margaret Hill, Richard Baggé, and Pat Miersma
in partnership with Good News Jail and Prison Ministry (goodnewsjail.org)

This book is intentionally written in basic English.

Unless otherwise noted, Scripture quotations are taken from the *Good News Translation® (Today's English Version, Second Edition)* © 1992 American Bible Society. All rights reserved. Passages marked **CEV** are from the *Contemporary English Version®* © 1995, 2006 American Bible Society. Bible stories are adapted from Scripture. Passages marked **NLT** are from the *Holy Bible, New Living Translation,* copyright © 1996, 2004, 2015 by Tyndale House Foundation. Used by permission of Tyndale House Publishers Inc., Carol Stream, Illinois 60188. All rights reserved.

Editor: Peter Edman
Design: Jordan Grove
Illustration: Ian Dale
Set in Post Grotesk.

For training in how to use this book to carry out trauma healing, see your local Bible Society, visit TraumaHealingInstitute.org, or write to traumahealing@americanbible.org.

Trauma Healing Institute

101 North Independence Mall East FL8
Philadelphia PA 19106–2155

Facilitator's Guide for Inmate Journal
© 2018 American Bible Society. Third edition, February 2019.
Editor: Dana Ergenbright. Design: Peter Edman

ISBN 978-1-58516-141-6-a (ABS item 124759)

Adapted from *Trauma Healing Classic Program Facilitator Manual* © 2016 American Bible Society

FACILITATOR'S GUIDE CONTENTS

FACILITATOR GUIDE TO THE INMATE JOURNAL F5

Welcome.. F7
If God loves us, why do we suffer? F9
How can the wounds of our heart heal?......................... F19
What happens when someone is grieving? F33
Taking your pain to the cross F45
How can we forgive others? F53
Looking back F63

PREPARING TO LEAD YOUR OWN HEALING GROUPS F69

Introduction F69
 Program overview F69
 Program model F69
 Program materials... F70

Facilitating Groups F72
 Participatory learning.................................... F72
 Using visual aids well F74
 Managing group dynamics F74
 Practice facilitation exercise F75

Healing Group Logistics F76
 Getting authorization F76
 Recruiting.. F76
 Preparing F76
 Reporting... F76
 Testimonies F78
 Healing group checklist F79

Orientation to Classic Trauma Healing Materials F79
Website.. F79
Next steps... F79
Action plan F79

APPENDIX F83

 I. Recruiting Session F83
 II. Healing group participation certificate F85
 III. Healing Group Report F86
 IV. Authorization for Testimonies & Recordings F87
 V. Healing Group Checklist F88
 VI. The Inmate edition of *Healing the Wounds of Trauma* ... F90
 VII. Reporting Requirements for Facilitators F92

CONTENTS

Welcome   7

If God loves us, why do we suffer?   9

How can the wounds of our heart heal?   19

What happens when someone is grieving?   33

Taking your pain to the cross   45

How can we forgive others?   53

Looking back   63

On your own   67

Facilitator Guide to the Inmate Journal

This is the table of contents for the *Inmate Journal*.

Page references in this handbook without a prefix ("page 5") are referring to the *Inmate Journal*, reproduced here.

Page references beginning with F ("page F5") are for the *Facilitator Guide*.

Confidentiality

Paraphrase: "The Bible repeatedly warns against gossip and indicates that a trustworthy person keeps a secret. The process of trauma healing requires a safe space for people to work through the materials and their own experiences. As a condition of your participation in this healing group, we ask that you not share information about others in the group—you can tell your story to anyone you wish, but you can only tell someone else's story with their permission. We also ask that you not share details about your case or anyone else's case.

"I also promise to keep confidential what you say. You already know, though, that there are certain things I have to report, like if someone is being abused or if a murder is going to happen."

(Note to facilitator: See appendix page F88 for more details)

Welcome (15 min)

Before you begin:
- Prepare name tent cards, if appropriate.
- Draw the diagram from p. 8 on the board/flip chart

WELCOME

Introduction

 DISCUSSION

What are your hopes for this group?

In this group, we'll be talking about the wounds of our hearts. Each lesson is interactive, and you may feel uncomfortable emotions at times— perhaps anger, sadness, anxiety, irritability, or tenseness. This is normal. It's part of the healing process, because we can't *heal* until we *feel*.

But you can choose if you want to participate and how much you are willing to share with others.

DISCUSSION

What should be the ground rules for our group?

_____

_____

_____

_____

_____

(1 min) Have everyone introduce themselves and tell the name they want to be called. Give out name tent cards, if appropriate. (Collect them at end of each class.)

(3 min) Discuss hopes for the group. Express this paragraph in your own words. Review table of contents (page 5 / page F5), as a brief overview of the class. Participants won't remember many details at this point. Keep it simple.

(6 min) Allow group to develop their own ground rules. Note:

- If they don't bring up confidentiality, be sure to introduce it (see opposite page).
- Healing groups are closed groups (i.e., visitors aren't allowed, and no new participants can join after group begins).
- Participants should come to all sessions. If someone has to miss a session, they should tell facilitators in advance. Another person can go over material with them before next meeting.

(5 min) Explain the diagram. Paraphrase the paragraph below it.

The healing journey

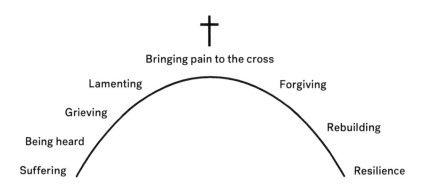

When people experience suffering and loss, their hearts can be wounded. For these wounds to heal, people need to express their pain to someone who listens to them without causing further harm. They need to accept the pain of the loss and grieve so that those feelings are not buried alive inside them. They can express these feelings honestly to God in lament. Once identified and expressed, they can bring that pain to Christ, who died on the cross for sin and everything sin brought with it: death, pain, sickness, conflict, abuse, and so forth. As we experience Christ's healing, we come to a place where we can begin to forgive those who have hurt us. We can begin to rebuild our lives and communities. We are better able to face suffering in the future.

F8

If God loves us, why do we suffer? (105 min)

Before you begin:

- Prepare slips of paper or index cards with Bible passages on p. 10.
- Choose which Bible passages you will use on p. 11 and 12.
- If using radio skit, make three copies, one for radio announcer, one for narrator, and one for listener.

Objectives:

By the end of this lesson we want to be able to:

- Identify false beliefs and teaching about God that can make our suffering more difficult.
- Explore problems with our earthly parents that keep us from experiencing the love of our heavenly Father.
- Begin to experience God's love in the midst of suffering.

(1 min) Introduce lesson title and objectives.

IF GOD LOVES US, WHY DO WE SUFFER?

1. The story of Ben

Ben grew up in the city of Las Palmas. He never knew his father. Until he was three, he was raised by his mom. Then she died and he had to go live with his aunt. Her husband was cruel to Ben. He beat Ben often and didn't give him enough to eat.

Ben went to school and made friends. When he was in middle school, one of his friends invited him to his church. Ben believed that Jesus had died for him, so he became a Christian. The church became like a family to him, and with the support of the pastor's family, Ben graduated from high school and got an associate's degree in substance abuse counseling. When he was just twenty-two, he got a job as an addictions counselor at a clinic in a town nearby. He got married and had two sons.

Over the years, gangs began to take control of his neighborhood in Las Palmas. Rival gangs had huge fights nearly every week. Ben saw innocent people being shot—children, women, passersby. Several of the young girls in his church had been gang raped. Other families were robbed at gunpoint. Las Palmas had become a war zone.

Ben was leaving work one day when he got the dreaded call: come to the emergency room! His five-year-old son Johnson had been hit by a stray bullet. By the time Ben got to the hospital, it was too late. The doctors were not able to save little Johnson's life.

Ben still goes to church and believes in the Bible, but he keeps asking why God has let him and his community suffer. He is angry with God and feels that God has deserted him. He has a hard time praying and his heart feels dead toward God. When he thinks of God as his Father, he can't imagine a loving father. In his experience, he only knew a father who was absent and an uncle who beat him cruelly.

Section 1 (15 min)

(5 min) Read story aloud or choose participant with high reading level. Instruct them to read with feeling.

(5 min) Small group. Have each group select someone to take notes and someone to speak for group (do this for each small group discussion going forward).

(5 min) Large group. Get feedback.

Section 2 (25 min)

(1 min) Paraphrase: "When we suffer, we try to make sense of our experience. What we know about God from the Bible might be different than what our culture tells us. This may cause us to doubt God's love for us."

(5 min) Small group. (9 min) Large group. Get feedback. List answers in left column, on board/flip chart.

> Common answers: God is: angry, far away, weak, punishing us, nonexistent.

(5 min) Small group. Give a Bible verse to each group, to read aloud in their group and discuss what it says about God's character.

(5 min) Large group. Get feedback. List answers in right column, on board/flip chart. Top up with content on next page.

> **Compare the two lists.** Emphasize that this is a tool to use whenever doubts about God's love arise.

One day he began to think of what he had been taught at school—that God didn't exist, that God did not create the world. Ben knew that this was not what the Bible teaches, but some part of him felt it might be true after all. Maybe there wasn't a God listening to his prayers.

Ben still takes his family to church and tries to teach his son about God, but he feels like a hypocrite because he talks about God's love, but he really feels God is far away.

 DISCUSSION

1. What is Ben feeling in his heart about God?
2. Why do you think Ben feels this way?
3. Have you ever felt like Ben?

2. When we are suffering, what do we need to remember about God's character?

DISCUSSION

What does the culture tell us about God, especially in times of suffering?

GOD'S CHARACTER	
Culture says ...	The Bible says ...
	Romans 8:35–39
	Psalm 34:18
	Genesis 6:5–6
	Matthew 9:35–36

Romans 8:35-39. God still loves us.

Sometimes when trouble comes we think it means God doesn't love us anymore. This is not true. Nothing can separate us from his love. God promises to always be with us, even when we suffer (Psalm 23:4-5; Hebrews 13:5b-6; Isaiah 43:1-2).

Psalm 34:18. God suffers with us and feels our pain.

Jesus understands our suffering because he suffered on the cross. His suffering was far beyond anything we will ever experience (Matthew 27:46; Hebrews 12:2-3). He suffers with those who are suffering (Matthew 25:35-36). He is merciful and gracious even when we have doubts (Isaiah 63:9; Isaiah 53:3-4; Hebrews 2:18).

Genesis 6:5-6. God hates evil and injustice.

Not everything that happens is the perfect will of God. God hates evil and injustice (Proverbs 6:16-19; Romans 1:18).

Matthew 9:35-36. Jesus looks for us when we are suffering and has compassion on us.

Jesus went looking for people who were suffering. He preached the Good News and healed people of all their diseases. He felt pity for them.

3. What is the origin of suffering in the world?

 DISCUSSION

How do *you* think suffering came into this world?

The Bible tells us:

1. Satan rebelled against God, and he wants to get as many people as he can to rebel against God (1 Peter 5:8-9; John 8:44).
2. When Adam and Eve chose to disobey God, evil and death entered the world (Genesis 3:1-24; Romans 5:12).
3. God gives all of us the freedom to choose whether we will obey him or not (Matthew 23:37b; Romans 3:10-18; Matthew 7:13-14). Sometimes, even though we obey God, we suffer because of other people's choices (1 Peter 2:20-22; 3:14-17).

Section 3 (20 min)

"Let's talk now about how suffering came into this world. Take a minute and write down how *you* think suffering came into this world."

(1 min) Individual. (2 min) Large group. Get feedback.

(17 min) "We are quick to blame God when bad things happen. Let's see what the Bible says about the origin of suffering in the world." Review the three points and write them on the board/flip chart, having participants read some of the verses aloud. Top up with content at bottom margin. Point out that we often do not know exactly why we are suffering.

Satan: Satan is a liar and murderer (John 8:44). Those who obey him lie, kill, and destroy. (See also Luke 22:31.)

Adam and Eve: Adam and Eve are the ancestors of all people. They chose to disobey God. When they did, evil and death entered the world (Genesis 3:1-24). All creation and all people experience the effects of Adam and Eve's disobedience (Romans 5:12; Romans 8:20-22). We can see these effects in natural disasters, people's behavior, disease, and so forth.

Freedom: God has given all people the freedom to choose good or evil. God is grieved when we choose to do bad things, but he lets us make our own choices (Matthew 23:37b, Romans 3:10-18).

Section 4 (33 min)

(1 min) "We talked about cultural beliefs that can make it hard to believe in God's goodness when we suffer. There are other things that can make it hard to believe, too."

(17 min) Large group. As you read each barrier aloud, ask "How might this make it hard to believe in God's goodness when we're suffering?" Get answers from group, then have someone read one or more of the verses aloud, time permitting. Top up with content on opposite page.

> *Alternative:* To introduce the first three barriers, do the radio skit (below) with narrator, radio announcer, and troubled listener. Then discuss the skit as a group, referring to first three barriers and biblical responses.

(10 min) Pairs. Tell participants when half the time has passed, so they can switch who is speaking.

(5 min) Large group. Get feedback. Keep to time limit.

4. What other things can make it difficult to believe in God's goodness when we suffer?

Barriers	Biblical responses	Notes
If we only hear about God's anger and judgment	Jeremiah 31:3 Lamentations 3:22–23 1 John 4:9–11	
If we are told that suffering means we haven't done enough to please God	Romans 5:8 Titus 3:4–6	
If we are taught that God promises prosperity for everyone who believes	Philippians 1:29 1 Peter 2:21 2 Corinthians 1:8–10	
If we do not do the things that will help our faith grow strong	John 8:31–32 2 Timothy 3:14–17 Acts 2:42 Hebrews 10:24–25	
Childhood experiences that make it difficult to believe in God's goodness	John 17:24 Romans 8:14–17 1 John 3:1	

🗨 DISCUSS IN PAIRS

Think about your own father. As a child, did you experience his love? Consider the same with your mother. How does your experience with your earthly parents affect your experience with your heavenly Father?

Radio skit

Narrator: A person has just experienced trauma *(for example, her son died after being seriously injured in a car accident).* She is overwhelmed and decides to listen to Christian radio for encouragement. A radio pastor on the first station she finds says:

Radio: "Do you have sin in your life? God knows—and he punishes sin! Repent before you fall into the hands of an angry God."

Listener: "Oh, I must have sinned. That's why this happened! God is angry with me. But what did I do? I don't know what to confess!"

Narrator: She decides to go to another station, where a radio pastor says:

Radio: "Jesus said, 'Fast and pray!' How much have you prayed today? How much have you fasted this week? How much money have you given to the church? Redouble your efforts and God will be pleased with you. He will answer your prayers."

If we only hear about God's anger and judgment.
It is true that God is all-powerful and judges sin, but we must also remember his great love for us (Jeremiah 31:3; Lamentations 3:22-23; 1 John 4:9-10).

If we are told that suffering means we haven't done enough to please God.
God's love is not based on our behavior. He loved us before we turned to him (Romans 5:8; Titus 3:4-5; 1 John 4:19). He continues to love us by grace, not because of what we do (Romans 3:23-24; Ephesians 2:8-9).

If we are taught that God promises prosperity for everyone who believes.
If we are taught that people who obey God will always be rich and healthy, we may feel guilty for suffering. We may feel that we have caused our own suffering by our lack of obedience and faith. The apostle Paul is a good example of someone who suffered a lot even though he was very obedient to God (2 Corinthians 1:8-10).

If we do not do the things that will help our faith grow strong.
As we follow Jesus and study the Bible, we learn the truth about God and this sets us free from the lies of Satan (John 8:31-32; 2 Timothy 3:14-17). Christians need to meet together for teaching, prayer, and fellowship (Acts 2:42; Philippians 4:6-7; Hebrews 10:24-25). If these things are missing, we will find it much harder to believe in God's goodness when we suffer.

Childhood experiences that make it difficult to believe in God's goodness.
Children need to feel secure and protected from evil. If we have experienced difficult things as a child, we may find it difficult to trust God when we become adults. For example, if we grew up without a father or mother, or if our father was often angry with us, then we may think God has abandoned us or that he is always angry with us, even though the Bible teaches us that God is a loving Father (John 17:24; Romans 8:14-17; 1 John 3:1).

Listener: "Oh, I have not done enough to please God. I should have prayed for two hours each morning, not just one. I should have fasted two days a week, not just one. And I should have found a way to give more money to the church. Then God would have blessed me. My son would not have died."

Narrator: She turns the dial once more and hears this:

Radio: "Hallelujah! If you have faith like a grain of mustard seed, you can say to this mountain—move to the sea, and it will be moved. Dear ones, do you have faith? Move that mountain in your life!"

Listener: "Oh, if only I had had more faith, my son would not have died. It's all my fault!"

(4 min) "I'd like to lead you through an exercise that can help you experience God's love."

Read the instructions and verses with sensitivity, pausing between each verse.

Leave time at end for them to silently talk to God.

» *Experiencing God's love*

It may be hard for you to receive love from God the Father because you view him through the lens of your earthly father. God our Father wants to give you pure and genuine love that will not hurt you in any way. Please receive that love as you reflect on these verses.

- **Lamentations 3:21-24.** *Yet hope returns when I remember this one thing: The LORD's unfailing love and mercy still continue, fresh as the morning, as sure as the sunrise. The LORD is all I have, and so in him I put my hope.*
- **1 John 3:1.** *See how much the Father has loved us! His love is so great that we are called God's children—and so, in fact, we are. This is why the world does not know us: it has not known God. My dear friends, we are now God's children, but it is not yet clear what we shall become. But we know that when Christ appears, we shall be like him, because we shall see him as he really is.*
- **Psalm 103:13.** *As a father is kind to his children, so the LORD is kind to those who honor him. He knows what we are made of; he remembers that we are dust.*
- **1 John 4:9-10.** *And God showed his love for us by sending his only Son into the world, so that we might have life through him. This is what love is: it is not that we have loved God, but that he loved us and sent his Son to be the means by which our sins are forgiven.*
- **1 Peter 5:7.** *Leave all your worries with him, because he cares for you.*

Taking care of yourself

When we start talking or thinking about the things we have experienced, we can begin to feel strong emotions. Remember, this is normal and is part of the healing process. There are many things we can do to take care of ourselves while we're healing.

» Breathing exercise

Breathing deeply can help us relax during strong emotions. If this makes you feel uncomfortable at any point, you can stop. You're in control.

- Get into a comfortable sitting position. (Later you can try this laying on your back.)
- Pick a spot on the wall and concentrate on it. Think only about your own breathing.
- Slowly breathe in and out, filling your lungs and slowly releasing the air. Imagine that you are pushing the breath to the wall and back. Think to yourself, "[Your name], feel yourself relaxing as oxygen is flowing in and out."
- Think about being in a quiet place. It might be the beach, or on a hill or in a tree. You might be alone or with someone who cares for you. You might think about Jesus telling you how much he loves you.
- Continue to think about your breathing, flowing in and out, in and out.
- After a few minutes, release your gaze from the spot on the wall. Stretch and take one more deep breath.

DISCUSSION

Was this helpful to you? Why or why not?

(4 min) Express this paragraph in your own words, then lead participants through the exercise.

(2 min) **Large group**. Get feedback.

Note: Some people who have experienced trauma feel more anxious when doing a breathing exercise. If a participant mentions this, tell them there are other exercises in this journal that they may find helpful.

(1 min) Give participants time to complete "Wrapping it up."

Wrapping it up

What's one thing you want to remember from this lesson?

Voices

I came to this Jail, not knowing what is going to happen in life. I wanted to start praying to allow God back into my life. While i was here i tried to pray. But I couldn't because I was in this unit. There were only a few Believers. I've ask if anyone had a bible; no-one answer me. And when I was going to give up, I seen this Daily Bread, so i ask if this belong to anyone. No-one said a word. So i took it to my room. Like a new book to Read. I then ask my friend if i could use his Book. He said O.K., but i seen a bible on the countertop. I grab it, and went to my room again. And now I ask God to help me. And come back into my life. Now have someone to teach me. My prayer's were answer. I got to come to this place called God's Mod. My life started to change, I meet some special people there.

There was this little woman that had this glow that I seen. She came up and told us she was going to start a class and see needed guy's to attend it. I wanted to go but the line on the paper was long. Never though I was going to get pick. Though all the other people were going to get pick first because they were here way befor me.

My friend said, Hey we were pick. Are you going to go. I said yes I going to be in this History Event. So here i am. i was not expected to do alot in class. But I was ready for anything. I felt like a Black Kettle there not knowing what the class is about or how hot its going to get. And when it got hot all these's emotion started poping up. I was scared at first. Did any-one see that Bubble pop up. Cry's loud cry's I couldn't explain it. Because when they poped, the word's were writ on my face. I tryed to keep my head down, so that no one could read them. But the tear's started to flow out. And then the tears were washing all my word's from my face.

I feel alot better now, I can say it is time to move on, and I don't have to let my emotion strike to the bottom any more. Thank you God for allowing your Angel Joy come into my life's. I will be going to court for a while. I just got out of leavenworth, KS. I was there for awhile. I prayed in the Sweat Lodge. And I went to the church on ever other Sunday. I work in there M-F day's. Keep my life Busy and had the Lord and the Great Father in my life. Sorry I gave them both up when I got out. Now I have the Lord back in my life. Thank you God.

17
If God loves us, why do we suffer?

Voices

How can the wounds of our heart heal?
(120 min, with art exercise as homework)

Before you begin:

- Write the "physical wound/heart wound" chart on board/flip chart, with the heart wound column blank (p. 22–23).
- If using the "pushing down emotions" skit, prepare index cards.
- Make copy of listening skit and rehearse.
- Prepare slips of paper or index cards with Bible passages on p. 29.
- Get extra paper for art exercise.

Objectives

By the end of this lesson we want to be able to:

- Explain how trauma is a "heart wound" and identify its symptoms.
- Show that God accepts our honest emotions.
- "Treat" heart wounds by talking and listening and by an art exercise.

HOW CAN THE WOUNDS OF OUR HEART HEAL?

(1 min) Introduce lesson title and objectives.

Taking care of yourself

Sometimes when we start thinking about the painful things we've experienced, we might feel like we're experiencing them again, like we're in the past rather than the present. When this happens, we can help ourselves by using our bodily senses to focus on the present moment.

» Senses exercise

Answer these questions in your mind, as a way to return yourself to the present.

- What are two things I can see?
- What are two things I can hear?
- What are two things I can feel?

Repeat the exercise, if needed, choosing additional things and describing them silently to yourself.

(3 min) Express this paragraph in your own words, then lead participants through the exercise. Pause between questions so participants can answer in their minds.

Note: If participants do not have an addiction history and will not be triggered by it, add the following questions to this exercise:

• What are two things I can smell?

• What are two things I can taste?

1. The fire

It was three in the morning when the phone rang in Laurel and Pete's bedroom. Laurel looked sleepily at Pete as he answered it, but became more alert as he started to get out of bed as he listened to the caller. "Bad fire," he said, "and it's coming this way!" Pete was a firefighter and Laurel was used to him being called out in the night, but somehow this seemed more serious than usual. Within five minutes Pete was out of the house on his way to the fire. Laurel wondered if she should wake the children, but first she went downstairs to turn on the television and find out what was happening.

Just as Laurel found a channel reporting on the fire, she heard cars driving outside, with loudspeakers telling everyone to get out. It took a while to get the three kids awake and dressed and into the car. As they left, clouds of smoke were getting nearer and they could even see the fire in the distance. Finally they arrived at a friend's house outside the danger zone. Laurel was so relieved to be safe, but then she began to worry about Pete.

There was no news for some hours but then Laurel got a message from a nearby hospital saying she should come at once because her husband was seriously hurt. As she rushed off, Laurel wondered if she would ever see Pete alive again. At the hospital, she heard that two other men in his unit had been killed and that Pete had burns on most of his body, his leg was crushed, and he had internal injuries. For three dreadful days, she thought he was going to die, but once they amputated his leg, he began to recover. It was a long time, though, before he could leave the hospital.

When he recovered, Pete was given a job in the office of the fire department. Laurel felt that things should be returning to normal but each week has seemed worse than the last. They both are having trouble sleeping and often have nightmares. But the worst part of it for Laurel has been Pete's personality change. Before the fire, he was generally a happy and balanced guy, but now he gets angry over little things. The children are beginning to be scared of their father because he yells at them when they make any noise. Laurel knows Pete is hurting inside because of the loss of his leg, but he won't talk about it because he thinks men should be strong. His friends just behave as though nothing has happened, but for Pete, his whole life has changed.

Laurel is becoming more and more depressed. She's lost interest in eating. It's especially hard for her at church because she is angry at God for not protecting her husband. Was God not able to protect him? Did God not care? What happened? Their pastor preaches that people who have strong faith in God are always H-A-P-P-Y and full of joy. Laurel knows this is not how she feels.

Finally Laurel talks to her small group leader, Pat. As she talks, she begins to cry and can't stop sobbing. It feels like pressure inside her has been released. Pat listens to Laurel tell what had happened. She asks Laurel to explain how she felt during the whole experience, and finally they talk about what the hardest part of the experience was for Laurel.

Laurel goes away feeling relieved. They have agreed to get together again for coffee the next week.

🗨 DISCUSSION

1. Besides the loss of Pete's leg, what else has he lost? What has Laurel lost? What do you think their children have lost?
2. In your area, what are some things people have lost?
3. What does your culture teach people to do with their emotions when they are suffering inside?

(5 min) Small group. Assign one question per group for discussion.

Goal of Q. 1 is to see how much was affected by one event (loss of security, beauty, economic ability, faith, health, sleep, happy home life, friends, job, etc.).

(5 min) Large group. Get feedback, listing answers to Q. 1 on board/flip chart.

Section 2 (28 min)

(2 min) Present definition of "heart wound." It can be effective to write "overwhelmed with" on board/flip chart, draw a large heart beneath it, and write inside the heart: "intense fear," "helplessness," "horror."

(3 min) Large group. Brainstorm sources of trauma. List on board/flip chart. Common answers: murder, rape, war, terrorism, car accidents, assault, earthquakes, floods, storms, wildfires, cancer, heart attacks.

(1 min) Present the question about incarceration as homework, to be discussed in participants' units.

(2 min) Large group. Briefly discuss physical wounds using these questions.

(9 min) Large group. Compare physical wound with heart wound. Write answers on board/flip chart. Have group fill in right column:

- Invisible, but shows up in behavior.

- Painful; must treat with care.

- Pain has to come out.

- If person pretends to be healed, it will cause greater problems.

- Only God heals, but uses people and understanding of how emotions heal.

2. What is a wound of the heart?

Our hearts can be wounded when we are overwhelmed with intense fear, helplessness, or horror. This is referred to as trauma. It can happen in the face of death, serious injury, rape, or other forced sexual activity. Sometimes witnessing trauma can be just as difficult as experiencing it.

 DISCUSSION

What are some sources of trauma? Consider those that are caused by humans as well as by nature.

DISCUSSION

How can incarceration contribute to trauma?

A heart wound is like a physical wound

 DISCUSSION

Think of a physical wound. How does it heal? What helps it heal?

How is a wound of the heart like a physical wound?

PHYSICAL WOUND	HEART WOUND
It is visible.	
It is painful and must be treated with care.	
It must be cleaned to remove any foreign objects/dirt.	
If a wound heals on the surface with infection still inside, it will cause the person to become very sick.	
Only God can bring healing, but he often uses people and medicine to do so.	

PHYSICAL WOUND	HEART WOUND
If not treated, it attracts flies.	
It takes time to heal.	
A healed wound may leave a scar.	

How do people with wounded hearts behave?

Proverbs 4:23 (NLT) tells us, *"Guard your heart above all else, for it determines the course of your life."* What happens to our heart affects how we live.

People with wounded hearts may behave in the following ways:

- **Reliving** the experience
- **Avoiding** reminders of the trauma
- **Being on alert** all the time

DISCUSSION

Think about wounded people you know. Have you seen anyone acting in these ways? Have you ever acted in these ways? Explain.

How would these things make someone feel?

(Heart wound, continued)

- If not treated, it attracts bad things.

- It takes time to heal.

- May leave a scar; person will not be the same.

(10 min) Present the three behaviors (see next page). List them on board/flip chart. Emphasize that these are normal reactions and may happen immediately or start a long time after event.

(1 min) Have participants write down their answers.

Reliving the experience

- thinking all the time about the event
- feeling like they're back in the event, while awake (flashbacks) or asleep (nightmares)
- telling everyone about what happened over and over again

This makes it hard to concentrate (i.e. at work or school).

Avoiding reminders of the trauma

- avoiding anything that brings back memories of event (i.e., places, people, emotions)
- going numb, not caring about what happens to them, not disturbed by violence or seeing dead bodies
- not remembering what happened, or only remembering parts of it
- using drugs or alcohol, or eating, working, or exercising too much, to avoid feeling the pain
- completely refusing to talk about it

Being on alert all the time

- always feeling tense, jumpy, frightened
- living in dread of another bad thing happening
- overreacting with violence or anger
- struggling to fall asleep, or waking up very early
- shaking, having a fast or irregular heartbeat
- having headaches and stomachaches
- feeling dizzy or faint, difficulty breathing, panic attacks

3. What does the Bible teach us about how to handle our feelings?

Some people who have troubles like these—even believers—say we shouldn't think or talk about our feelings. They say we should just forget the past and move on. They think that feeling pain in our hearts means we are doubting God's promises. This is not true! Here are some Bible passages that address strong feelings.

- Matthew 26:37-38 (Jesus)
- John 11:33-35 (Jesus)
- Matthew 26:75 (Peter)
- Jonah 4:1-3 (Jonah)
- 1 Samuel 1:10, 13-16 (Hannah)
- Psalm 55:4-6 (David)

Jesus had strong feelings and shared them with his disciples. Paul teaches us to share our problems with each other as a way of caring for each other (Galatians 6:2; Philippians 2:4). The Old Testament is full of examples of people pouring out their hearts to God. The writer of one psalm told God, *"I am hurt to the depth of my heart"* (Psalm 109:22). God wants us to be honest and speak the truth from our hearts.

 **DISCUSSION**

In your family, how do you handle emotions?

4. How can we heal from the wounds of our hearts?

One way we can begin to heal is by talking about our pain. Usually we need to talk to another person about our pain before we are ready to talk to God about it. We may need to tell our story many times. If we are able to talk about our bad experiences, then after a while our reactions will become less and less intense. But if we are not able to talk about our pain, and if there is no one to help us, these reactions may continue for months and even years.

Section 3 (22 min)

(1 min) Mention section title and express first paragraph in your own words.

(4 min) Small group. Assign verses to groups. Have them discuss what their verse teaches about handling our emotions.

(10 min) Large group. Get feedback, and top up with this paragraph.

(5 min) Small group.
(2 min) Large group.
Get feedback. Keep to time limit.
Note: If you have 5 minutes extra, do the "pushing down emotions" skit (next page).

Section 4 (40 min)

(1 min) Mention section title and express paragraph in your own words. Time permitting, paraphrase "Trauma and the brain" content (below).

(6 min) Listening skit (see next page). Then discuss what they observed.

Trauma and the brain

Trauma disconnects. It disconnects the person from themselves, from others, and from God. Even within their own brain, there is disconnection. Reconnection begins when people tell the story differently in a safe environment. They can associate new memories with it.

Pushing down emotions skit

(5 min) (Courtesy Carolyn Turner)

Prior to class, write different emotions on index cards (one emotion per card), such as shock, fear, grief, anger, depression, rage, anxiety, confusion, guilt, sadness, etc. Prepare one fewer card than the number of participants.

Select one participant to be a person who experienced a traumatic event. Have that person cover their ears and close their eyes so that directions may be given to the other participants. Give each remaining participant one index card; this ensures that everyone in your group may participate in the skit. Instruct these participants that they will periodically stand up, and when the person taps their shoulder, they will sit down.

Have the "traumatized person" stand at the front of the room and tell them more details about the traumatic event they experienced (i.e., "Imagine that while you were in jail you were called to the chaplain's office and received news that your house had burned down to the ground. All the people and animals had gotten out safely but you had lost everything else—furniture, clothes, pictures, a place to live.

Even your car that was parked in the garage was burned, beyond recognition."). Then have one person stand up with their emotion card, such as the "shock" card. Explain to the traumatized person that the only way he or she knows how to deal with the emotion is to push it down or, in this case, to tap the person holding the card on the shoulder. The person that is tapped must sit back down for the time being.

When that "emotion" sits down, other participants should randomly pop up from their seats, holding their cards. The traumatized person will tap them on the shoulders, to "push down the emotions." (Reminder: When a person is tapped on the shoulder he/she should sit back down, but then pop back up again in a few seconds.) This process will be repeated numerous times. The traumatized person is then moving quickly around the room to "push down the emotions." The skit should continue for at least two or three minutes so that everyone feels the stress and fatigue of pushing emotions down and not dealing with them.

After the skit, debrief and ask the traumatized person how he or she felt, and then ask the other participants. Mention that it takes a lot of energy to push down our emotions. It becomes impossible for us to focus on anything else. We need to let the pain out to heal.

Listening skit (Bad listening vs. good listening)

Michael was in a bad car accident a week ago which left him with a broken arm and minor concussion, nearly killed his wife and child, and killed the driver of the other car. He has been able to go home from the hospital but is worried about his family. Although he has people to help him with meals, housework, and getting to and from the hospital for visits, he is feeling worse and worse. His pastor, Paul, has just stopped at the hospital to visit Michael's wife and daughter. He finds Michael in the waiting area, pacing back and forth. (P = Pastor Paul; M = Michael)

Bad listening

P: (Rushed greeting) I came to see your family.

M: They're sleeping just now, but I'm not doing so well.

P: Look at the positive: you survived! Thank God! (rushed)

M: But I'm feeling confused. Could we talk?

P: (distracted) I have a building committee meeting. Let's talk as we walk to my car.

M: Okay (reluctantly). Now that my wife and daughter are okay, I'm feeling worse. I'm not sleeping and I'm avoiding cars and especially driving.

P: There's no reason to be afraid. Forget it. Take control. God hasn't given us a "spirit of fear."

M: Oh no! Now I feel guilty about feeling afraid. And I feel angry. I know I should feel thankful, but . . .

P: Yes! You should be thankful. Being thankful will wipe away the negative feelings. This reminds me of when our church burned down. I decided to rejoice, and everything was fine.

M: I tried to, but I can't control the fear. (P's phone rings)

P: (answers his phone and says) "I'm talking with Michael. He's having a really hard time, but I'll be there as soon as I can get away."

M: I can see you're busy, but what can I do about this fear?

P: Remember Romans 8:28. Be thankful. I'll ask the church to pray for you.

M: Oh please no, don't tell everyone!

P: Don't worry—we're a family. It's all in the family. There's no reason to be embarrassed. I've gotta run.

M: (dejected)

Good listening

P: Greeting. Came to see you.

M: Thanks! I'm not doing so well.

P: Do you want to talk? Let's go somewhere private.

M: Okay.

P: Tell me what happened.

M. It's a horrible scene in my head. We were going up a hill, a car came over the hill into our lane, speeding. There was no time to react. I swerved and spun and ended up in a ditch upside down. I smelled gas. My wife and daughter were unconscious and bleeding. I got out and was screaming for my family. I managed to get them out from under the car. I was afraid the gas would explode.

P: It's amazing you could think clearly. Were you in pain?

M: I don't know. It was a blurry nightmare. I think I was in shock.

P: How did you feel?

M: I was worried about our new suitcases. I know that sounds crazy.

P: That's not crazy. Maybe it kept you from being over-whelmed.

M: I hadn't thought about it like that.

P: Tell me more.

M: Well, first I was glad to have survived, but now I have bad thoughts and feelings. I'm confused. I felt so helpless and wanted to kill the driver. He died, but I wish I could have killed him myself. I shouldn't feel this way.

P: I'd probably fewel that way, too.

M: Really? Helpful to hear. I just don't feel thankful, even though my family survived. I'm not sleeping well. I know cars are probably safe, but I'm afraid of them anyway. I'm feeling very angry for no reason. I should feel thankful my family is recovering, right?

P: Well, it's normal to have all these feelings after what you've been through. What was the hardest thing for you?

M: The worst was seeing my daughter and wife injured.

P: Yeah. You said you felt helpless?

M: Totally. I'm a man, you know, and I couldn't do anything.

P: What helped you cope so far?

M: My family needs me.

P: Yeah. We love you too. We can talk again next week, okay?

M: Thanks. It really helps to talk about it. Do you want to see my family? They're awake now.

P: Yes, let's.

(1 min) State section title, then present bullet points.

A. What begins to happen when we talk about our pain?

When we talk with someone who knows how to listen:

- We can gain an honest understanding of what happened and how it has affected us.
- We can accept what happened.
- We can feel heard and know we are not alone.
- We can become able to trust and rest in God, and let God begin to heal our hearts (see Psalm 62:8 and Psalm 103:3).

(12 min) State section title, then large group discussion question. List feedback on board/flip chart. Add content that has not been mentioned from the four marks of a good listener (page 26–27).

B. What is a good listener like?

 **DISCUSSION**

With what kind of person would you feel free to share your deep pain?

1. Creates a safe space

For us to share the deep wounds of our hearts with someone, we need to know that our listener:

- Cares about us.
- Will keep the information confidential.
- Will listen and understand our pain.
- Will not criticize us or give quick solutions.
- Will not minimize our pain by comparing it with their own pain.

2. Asks helpful questions

Here are three helpful questions to guide us when we are sharing our pain or listening to others:

- What happened?
- How did you feel?
- What was the hardest part for you?

Rationale for three questions:

- **Q1:** Establishes facts and timeline, which get jumbled in our brains during a traumatic event.
- **Q2:** Since healing takes place at the level of emotions, it helps to name them.
- **Q3:** Each person is different, so we should not assume we know the answer.

3. Shows they are listening to us

- Looks at us, not out the window, at their watch, or at their phone.
- Doesn't seem impatient for us to finish.
- Says words of agreement like "Mmm."
- From time to time, repeats what they think we've said (so we can correct, restate, or affirm their understanding).

26
Healing the Wounded Heart

4. Respects the healing process

- Notices if we become very distressed and knows it's not helpful to continue. Lets us take a break, think about other things, and get calm inside. We can resume telling our story when we feel ready.
- May gently ask us if we would like prayer. If we say "yes," the listener prays but does not preach. If we say "no," the listener honors this.

» Listening exercise, in pairs

Talk about one bad thing that happened to you—a small thing, not the worst thing you've experienced. The other person listens, using the three questions above. Then switch roles.

Afterward, discuss these questions as a group:

- How did you feel during this exercise?
- Was anything difficult?
- Did you feel heard when you were listened to? Why or why not?
- What did the listener do well?

(15 min) Pairs. Explain the listening exercise and have participants pair up. Give each person 6–7 minutes to talk, while the other listens, then switch roles.

(5 min) Large group. Discuss the bulleted questions.

(2 min) Paraphrase content.

C. Serious cases

Certain things make heart wounds more serious ...

- Something very personal, for example, a family member dying or being betrayed by a close friend
- Something that goes on for a long time
- Something that happens many times over a period of time.
- Something connected with death
- Something that people have done intentionally to cause pain rather than something that is accidental

People react to painful events differently. Two people may go through the same event, but one may have a severe reaction while the other is not affected much at all. A person is likely to react more severely to trauma if he or she:

- always wants someone else to tell them what to do.
- has mental illness or emotional problems.
- is usually sad or is sensitive.
- had many bad things happen in the past, particularly if they happened when he or she was a child, like both parents dying.
- already had many problems before this happened.

» Art exercise

Another way we can get the pain in our hearts out without using words is by drawing. Start by getting quiet inside and asking God to show you the pain in your heart. Begin drawing one of your painful experiences without thinking about it too much. Try to let the pain come out through your fingers. The senses exercise and the breathing exercise can help you if you feel very strong emotions during this exercise.

🗨 DISCUSSION

1. Share as much or as little as you'd like about your drawing. Or, if you'd prefer, share what the experience was like of drawing your pain.
2. Was there anything new you realized about your situation?

(5 min) Explain exercise and assign as homework. Distribute blank paper, so participants have option of drawing either in their journal or on paper. Encourage them to spend at least 20–30 minutes doing the exercise.

Time permitting, explain that our brains record traumatic events in a different way than normal events. The part of the brain that puts words to events and makes sense of them goes "offline" during a traumatic event. When it comes back "online" after the event, it has a hard time making sense of what happened and describing it. Art can access these memories that haven't been put into words yet, and enables them to be expressed.

At the beginning of the next lesson, use these questions to debrief the art exercise.

(4 min) Lead participants through this section. Remind them that they can use these exercises outside of class, to help them deal with strong emotions. They can also teach them to other inmates.

(1 min) Give participants time to complete "Wrapping it up." Assign homework:

- Art exercise
- Discussion question ("How can incarceration contribute to trauma?")

Taking care of yourself

Do the senses exercise and the breathing exercise before you leave.

What's one thing you will do to take care of yourself today?

Wrapping it up

What's one thing you want to remember from this lesson?

Voices

Oh God

Why do I continue to struggle with everything, why do I continue to loose the war Ive been fighting with my addictions to drugs and anger? Why do you not help me when I start to fall, Why do you seperate me and my family.

I love my family. I love my girl and my little girl so much and you took me away from them. Now I have to spend the rest of my life away from them. I wont get to see my children grow up. I wont get to teach my son how to be a man. I wont get to watch my daughter blossom in to a woman. My children will grow to hate me!

I ask you for mercy lord. I beg you for mercy in the court room.

I ask you to take this away from me God. I beg you please God let me be the father I need to be. Let me be the father my children deserve, even if your will is for me to raise my children from prison. God I trust and believe you are working in my life. God I trust in you and you are a god of mercy. I have never stopped believing that you are my lord and saviour. I have given my life to you, and I understand and have faith in your will, and your will will be done and I am fine with that.

Regardless of the outcome I will continue to praise you, I will continue to bring more and more of your sheep to you. I will stay in the word and spread your word lord. I love you lord

Love your Son

What happens when someone is grieving? (120 min, with art exercise debrief and lament exercise assigned as homework)

Before you begin:

- Draw grief journey on board/flip chart.
- Get extra paper for lament exercise.
- If you plan to use trifold paper activity for grief journey, bring extra paper and colored pencils/pens/crayons.

Objectives

By the end of this lesson we want to be able to:

- Recognize that all trauma involves grief and that we need to grieve in order to heal.
- Understand the different stages of grief and respond well to each one.
- Express our pain to God through lament, as an important part of grieving.

WHAT HAPPENS WHEN SOMEONE IS GRIEVING?

Discuss homework:

(20 min) Art exercise. Invite participants to share, in small or large group, using questions on p. 26.

(10 min) Discussion question: "How can incarceration contribute to trauma?"

(1 min) Introduce lesson title and objectives.

(3 min) Introduce content, then lead participants through the container exercise.

Taking care of yourself

Sometimes we can be overwhelmed by what we have experienced but we are not in a situation where we can express how we feel. This exercise can be helpful.

» *Container exercise*

Close your eyes or look down at the floor so you are not distracted. Imagine a big container. It could be a big box or a shipping container. Imagine a way to lock the container, like a key or a padlock.

Now imagine putting all the things that are disturbing you right now into the container: big things, small things—everything that is disturbing you. When they are all inside the container, close it. Now lock the container and put the key somewhere safe. Do not throw it away. When you are ready, open your eyes and look up.

Later, find a time when you can get quiet. Take the key and open the container, then one by one take out the things you have put inside. You may want to do this with someone who can help you talk about these things. Do not leave them in the container forever!

1. The night that changed Tony's life

Tony was home with his family after a long day at school and work. He lived on the "bad" side of town—if you weren't from there you would never go there, except by accident. Tony lived in a cramped one-bedroom apartment with his two younger brothers and his mom. He had goals to get his GED and help his mom raise his brothers. He worked hard to stay out of trouble and to avoid the gangs that so many of his friends had joined.

One night Tony took an extra shift at the pizza place where he worked, so he didn't get off until 11 p.m. The busy corner where he lived was on the line dividing two opposing gangs in his neighborhood. They were continually fighting for control of this neutral street.

On this night, a terrible battle broke out right in front of Tony's house. His mom was on her way home from picking up his brothers and they found themselves in the middle of it. His youngest brother was shot and killed immediately, and Joe, his other brother, was seriously wounded and taken to the hospital.

Tony came home to see police tape on the scene, and police everywhere. His neighbor got to him first and told him what happened. Tony ran toward the house, pushing wildly through the crowd. When a police officer tried to stop him, Tony punched him. The officer cuffed him, wrestled him to the police car, and booked him on assault.

In the jail, Tony's grief began to overwhelm him. He found himself crying when no one was looking. This made him feel embarrassed and he tried hard to hold in his feelings. He began losing sleep and was tormented with thoughts of guilt and regret. "If only I had been there, I could have stopped it!" Over and over again these thoughts ran through his mind. He also began to plot revenge on the gang members who had destroyed his family.

Because he had not been sentenced he was not able to furlough to his brother's funeral. He felt enraged at everyone—the officer who arrested him, the gang members, the attorney for not arranging a furlough, God for letting all this happen. When he didn't feel enraged, he felt numb, like he was walking through fog. "I can't believe this is happening to me."

 DISCUSSION

1. What has Tony lost?
2. What are some things you have lost as a result of being incarcerated?

2. What is grieving?

Grieving is feeling the loss of something.

 DISCUSSION

What kind of losses can we grieve?

Grieving is part of the normal process of recovering from loss. When we lose someone or something important to us, we may also lose a sense of who we are. As we grieve, our sense of who we are gradually changes and we adjust to our new stage of life. This takes time.

When Adam and Eve sinned, death came into the world—and with it the need for grieving. Only in heaven will there be no more pain and grief (Revelation 21:4).

(5 min) Large group. Discuss Question 1, and briefly refer to Question 2. Keep to time limit.

Section 2 (5 min)

(2 min) Large group. Define grieving, then discuss question. List answers on flip chart/board

Common answers: family member, friend, body part, function of part of body, sense of safety, innocence, property, position

(3 min) Express these paragraphs in your own words. Then draw and explain the "trauma/grief" diagram:

All trauma involves grief, as it involves loss of some sort. But we can experience grief without trauma (for example, the slow death of an elderly parent). Not all emotional pain is trauma, and not all problem behaviors are the result of trauma.

F35

Section 3 (30 min)

(15 min) Present the grief journey, either drawn on board/flip chart, or using the trifold paper activity (see below) or the grief journey script (see p. F37b). As you present each camp, involve the participants by asking "What would you be saying to yourself in this camp? What would you be feeling?"

3. How can we grieve in a way that brings healing?

The grief journey

Grieving takes time and energy. It is like a journey that requires stops at several camps, but leads to healing (Isaiah 61:1–3).

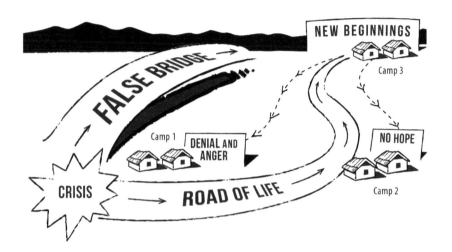

Camp 1: Denial and Anger
(often 1 month or longer)

Right after a loss, denial and anger are natural and can actually be helpful in some ways:

- Denial allows us to absorb the loss little by little and keep us from being over-whelmed by it.

- Anger can be a way of fighting against the loss when we feel helpless. It can give us energy and keep us from being overwhelmed.

This stage can begin during the time of the funeral, and while people are still coming to comfort the bereaved family. Weeping and rituals of the wake and burial are often helpful.

Camp 1: Denial and Anger

- Numb
- Not aware of what is happening around us
- Can't believe the person has died or the event has happened
- May suddenly start to cry or erupt in anger
- May be angry with God
- May be angry with a person who has died, for leaving us alone
- "If only I had done this or that, the person wouldn't have died" or "I wish I had …"
- "Why did this happen to me?"
- May find someone to blame for the death
- May take revenge, which results in conflict and more pain
- May think we hear or see the dead person

Trifold paper activity

(Courtesy Becky Botts)

Have each participant fold an 8.5×11 sheet of paper in thirds, horizontally, so it can fold into a standing triangle. On each of the three flat surfaces have them briefly draw one of the three camps. As the discussion proceeds, camp by camp, they can write on the corresponding camp the emotions felt in that camp. If colored pencils are allowed, they can choose a different color for each camp. You can also have the participants "strike a pose" of one emotion in each camp, showing it on their face and by their body language. When the discussion turns to backtracking to Camp 1 and 2 during the grief process, the triangle can be turned.

Camp 2: No Hope

- Sad and hopeless
- Hard to organize life
- Long for the dead person to come back
- May feel lonely
- May want to kill ourselves
- May feel guilty even if there is no reason to

Camp 3: New Beginnings

- Think about moving on to a new life
- Ready to go out with friends and have fun
- May consider remarrying if a spouse died, or having another child if a child died
- Changed by the loss; may be stronger, more tender

Backtracks and the 'false bridge'

The grief journey is not always direct. It is normal for people to revisit previous camps for a short period of time. Sometimes this happens in response to an event like the anniversary of a death.

It is tempting to try to bypass the process of grieving. We want to start over without dealing with our feelings about our loss, but this is not healthy. The grief will stay inside us and cause problems for many years. The **"false bridge"** is a dead end.

DISCUSSION, IN PAIRS

1. Think of a loss you have experienced. How would you describe that time?
2. In your grief journey, have you looped back or gotten stuck along the way? Explain.
3. Have you tried to take the false bridge to avoid feeling the pain of loss? Explain.

Camp 2: No Hope
(often 6–15 months; may last longer)

Camp 2 is the darkest place in the grieving process. People don't expect anything good to follow.

Camp 3: New Beginnings

In Camp 3, people increasingly accept the loss and their new identity. What is "normal" now is different—a "new normal." They may be more aware of what really matters in life. If they have grieved well, they may be able to help others.

Backtracks and 'false bridge'

See note about "Getting stuck" (below).

(10 min) Pairs. Tell participants when half the time has passed, so they can switch who is speaking.

(5 min) Large group. Get feedback.

Getting stuck

Sometimes people get stuck too long in Camp 1 or 2, and may need special help to move on. For example,

- A woman may still think she can see or hear her husband a year after he is dead.
- A mother of a dead child may keep his clothes ready for him, and won't give them away a year or more after the death.
- A man may still be unwilling to go to social events with his friends two years after his wife has died.

Grief Journey script

Note to facilitator: Acting out the grief journey is an important visual learning tool, but how it is done will depend on the size of the group. The three villages of Anger and Denial, No Hope, and New Beginnings need to be marked with a sign at three places in the room. Options for marking the villages are putting signs on the wall, signs on chairs, or have one or a group of people at each village holding a sign.

It's important for people to dramatize the different thoughts and emotions. If the people are shy and hesitant, the facilitator should lead in acting the anger, denial, etc. at each village; usually the participants readily join in.

With a small group, you can take all the participants on the journey between the three villages. With a larger group, have five people move through the villages.

Taking the journey

Have five volunteers come to the front of the room. State a hypothetical disaster (for example, they are a family whose mother/wife has just died in a car accident).

Village 1: Denial and Anger

Say: **Immediately after the disaster, the family is in Village 1, the Village of Denial and Anger. This often lasts 1 month or longer.**

Ask: **How do people in Village 1 feel?**

Get responses. Add anything they don't say from the list below. Explain that the behavior is normal in each camp as a person goes from crisis to recovery.

- Numb
- Not aware of what is happening around us
- Can't believe the person has died or the event has happened
- May suddenly start to cry or erupt in anger
- May be angry with God
- May be angry with a person who has died, for leaving us alone
- "If only I had done this or that, the person wouldn't have died" or "I wish I had ..."
- "Why did this happen to me?"
- May find someone to blame for the death
- May take revenge, which results in conflict and more pain
- May think we hear or see the dead person

Say (and act): **Persons A and B are very angry at the people who caused the event and want revenge now! They get angry with anyone who walks in the room and shout at them.** [Encourage A and B to act in this way, and so on, with the description of each subsequent person.] **Person C is very angry at himself because he thinks he could have prevented the disaster. Person D is very angry at God for permitting this to happen. Person E is saying that his wife isn't really dead, they will be reunited soon.**

Say: **Right after a loss, denial and anger are natural and can actually be helpful in some ways. Denial allows us to absorb the loss little by little and keep us from being overwhelmed by it. Anger can be a way of fighting against the loss when we feel helpless. It can give us energy and keep us from being overwhelmed.**

Village 2: No Hope

Say: **At a certain point, we may come to Village 2, the Village of No Hope. This often lasts between 6–15 months, although it can be different for each person.**

Ask: **How do people in the Village of No Hope feel?**

Get responses. Add anything they don't say from the list below. Explain that the behavior is normal in each camp as a person goes from crisis to recovery.

- Sad and hopeless
- Hard to organize life
- Long for the dead person to come back
- May feel lonely
- May want to kill ourselves
- May feel guilty even if there is no reason to

Say (and act): **Person A stays in Anger and Denial because they are still very angry and thinking about revenge.** [Encourage A to act in this way, and so on, with the description of each subsequent person.] **Persons B, C, and D no longer feel as much anger and they go to the camp of No Hope. E accepts that the loved one is dead because of going through the funeral, and goes to No Hope. Suddenly Person C sees something that reminds them of the initial event, and that triggers more anger.** [Facilitator walks back with C to Denial and Anger to join A.]

Say: **After a few weeks A and C find that their anger is calming down, and they join the others at No Hope. They all feel sad, they are not interested in life.**

Say: **Village 2 is the darkest place in the grieving process. People don't expect anything good to follow.**

Village 3: New Beginnings

Say: **At a certain point, we may come to Village 3, the Village of New Beginnings. How do people in the Village of New Beginnings feel?**

Get responses. Add anything they don't say from the list below.

- Think about moving on to a new life
- Ready to go out with friends and have fun
- May consider remarrying if a spouse died, or having another child if a child died
- Changed by the loss; may be stronger, more tender

Say (and act): **Ten months after the crisis, D and E start to feel more interest in life. They go to New Beginnings.** [Encourage D and E to act in this way, and so on, with the description of each subsequent person.] **They start to join in activities with their friends. But A, B and C still feel sad** and lonely in No Hope. Twelve months after the disaster, B and C also go to New Beginnings. But A stays in No Hope, still longing for the person who died. On Christmas, however, B, C, and D have painful memories of how Christmas used to be, and they go for a time back to No Hope. Then, at fifteen months they all move to New Beginnings to join Person E.

Say: **In Camp 3, people increasingly accept the loss and their new identity. What is "normal" now is different than what was normal before the loss—a "new normal." They may be more aware of what really matters in life and may be more tender.**

Say: **Every one of the five people's journeys was different. Each individual spends different amounts of time in the villages and goes back and forth at different times.**

False Bridge

Now a different disaster has just happened, and Person A is at Anger and Denial.

Say: **What if someone comes and takes the hand of Person A and pulls them immediately to New Beginnings, saying, "Don't be angry, don't be sad. If you trust God, you can feel happy right now. Just resume your life as though nothing has happened?"** [Act this out with participant A] **What do you think will happen to Person A?**

Possible answers: It will be like the pushing emotions down skit, will feel ashamed for having negative feelings, will feel like a failure spiritually, etc.

Say: **The problem with the false bridge is that it does not work. The grief will stay inside us and cause problems for many years.**

Section 4 (8 min)

(1 min) "Grieving is hard work, but some things can make it even more difficult, like how the loss happened or beliefs people have about grief."

(2 min) Present types of loss.

(5 min) Large group. Get feedback, then top up with the content in the bullets that follow.

4. What can make grieving more difficult?

The type of loss

- When there are too many deaths or losses at the same time
- When the death or loss is sudden and unexpected
- When the death or loss is violent
- When there is no body to be buried or no way to confirm that the person has died
- When the person that provided for the family has died
- When we had unresolved problems with the dead person
- When the death is a suicide or murder
- When a child has died

Cultural beliefs about weeping

 DISCUSSION

What does your culture or family think about men weeping? What does it say about women weeping?

Culture and weeping

- If our culture or family doesn't allow us to cry, we'll hold our grief inside rather than letting it out.
- God has designed us to cry or weep when we are sad. It's an important part of grieving, for men as well as women.
- Even Jesus wept when his close friend Lazarus died (John 11:33-38a). The psalmists wept (Psalm 6:6; 39:12; 42:3), as did the prophets (Isaiah 22:4; Jeremiah 9:1). Ecclesiastes 3:4 says there is a time to weep.
- God notices our tears; they are precious to him (Isaiah 38:3-5).

5. What helps us when we are grieving?

💬 DISCUSSION, IN SMALL GROUPS

1. When you have been mourning the loss of someone or something, what sort of helpful things have people done or said?
2. What sort of unhelpful things have people done or said?

What helps when we're grieving?

- People who listen to our pain, who do more listening than talking. We cannot absorb teaching and sermons at this time (Job 21:2; Proverbs 18:13).
- People who help us with practical things, at time of funeral but also in following months and years.
- Reminding ourselves that it is normal to grieve, and that it is a process that will take time. We will not always feel like we do today.
- Avoiding big decisions and major changes, like marrying someone. When we are in Camp 3, we will be able to make better decisions.
- Getting exercise and wearing ourselves out physically, so we can sleep better. It's common to have difficulty sleeping in the weeks and months after a loss.
- Reading the psalms, especially the laments. These can provide great comfort.
- Bringing our losses to the Lord, one by one. The more specific we can be, the better.

Section 5 (12 min)

(5 min) Mention section title. **Small group.** Have some groups discuss Question 1 and others discuss Question 2.

(7 min) Large group. Get feedback, listing answers on flip chart/board, then top up with content below.

Time and context permitting, paraphrase Job paragraph from bottom margin.

Note: If inmates have lost a family member while they're incarcerated, hold a service to honor the deceased. Bring a copy of the obituary and a photograph, and have the inmate write a eulogy. Include prayer, Bible verses, and a eulogy in the service.

Job

Job was a wealthy man with a large family. In an instant, he lost everything: his children, his cattle, his wealth, his health. When his friends heard about Job's problems, they came to comfort him. They sat in silence with him for a week before speaking. Then Job broke the silence by expressing his pain. His friends were quick to point out his lack of faith (Job 4:3–6), and that his suffering was due to his sins and the sins of his children (Job 4:7–8). Although Job claimed he had not sinned, they were sure that if he were innocent God would not have let this happen (Job 8:6–8; 11:2–4; 22:21–30). They accused him over and over to try to get him to confess. Finally Job said, "Miserable comforters are you all!" (Job 16:2 NIV). Rather than comforting Job, they increased his pain.

Laments (15 min)

(10 min) Present this content. Bring out that the only part that must be present in a lament is the complaint.

Laments

One of the tools we can use to help us grieve is lament. In a lament, people pour out their complaints to God and ask God to act on their behalf, often while stating their hope or trust in God.

Laments in the Bible can have the following parts.

- Address to God ("O God")
- Review of God's faithfulness in the past
- **A complaint**
- A confession of sin or claim of innocence
- A request for help
- God's response (often not stated)
- A vow to praise God or a statement of trust in God

Not all parts are present in each lament, and they are not always in the same order. The only essential part is the complaint.

A lament allows a person to fully express their grief and even accuse God, but this is often followed by a statement of trust in God. This combination makes for a very powerful prayer. The grief is not hidden, but the person does not stay in their grief—they call on God and try to express their trust. The laments encourage people be honest with God, to speak the truth about their feelings and doubts. To lament to God is a sign of faith, not doubt.

In a lament, people do not attempt to solve the problem themselves, but they cry to God for help. They look to God, not an enemy or random chance, as the one ultimately in control of the situation. They ask God to take action to bring justice rather than taking action themselves or cursing the enemy.

Psalm 13	Lament part
[1] How much longer will you forget me, LORD? Forever? How much longer will you hide yourself from me? [2] How long must I endure trouble? How long will sorrow fill my heart day and night? How long will my enemies triumph over me?	Address and complaint
[3] Look at me, O LORD my God, and answer me. Restore my strength; don't let me die. [4] Don't let my enemies say, "We have defeated him." Don't let them gloat over my downfall.	Request
[5] I rely on your constant love;	Statement of trust in God
I will be glad, because you will rescue me. [6] I will sing to you, O LORD, because you have been good to me.	Vow to praise

*Sixty-seven of the Psalms are considered laments—more than any other type of psalm. Some were for use by individuals; others were used by the community together. The individual lament Psalms are: 3, 4, 5, 6, 7, 9-10, 11, 13, 16, 17, 22, 25, 26, 27, 28, 31, 35, 36, 38, 39, 40, 42, 43, 51, 52, 54, 55, 56, 57, 59, 61, 62, 63, 64, 69, 70, 71, 77, 86, 88, 94, 102, 109, 120, 130, 140, 141, 142, 143. The community lament Psalms are: 12, 14, 44, 53, 58, 60, 74, 79, 80, 83, 85, 90, 106, 108, 123, 126, 137.

» Write a lament

Take some time to create a lament to God. Read Psalm 13 as an example. Your lament could be a song, rap, poem, prayer, or any creative way you wish to express your feelings to God. It does not have to include all parts of a lament, but it does need to have a complaint.

(3 min) Read Psalm 13 together, identifying lament parts. You can ask participants to cover the "lament part" column on right with their hands, and try to identify the part themselves.

(2 min) Explain exercise, and assign as homework. Distribute blank paper, so participants have option of writing either in their journal or on paper. Encourage them to spend at least 20-30 minutes writing it.

Use this space or a separate sheet of paper to write your lament.

At the beginning of the next lesson, use this discussion to debrief the lament exercise.

 DISCUSSION, IN SMALL GROUPS

Share as much or as little as you'd like of your lament. Or share what the process of writing a lament was like for you.

Taking care of yourself

It can be hard to go right back into your cell or unit after opening up so many strong emotions. Do the container exercise again to help you put some things "back in the box" until later, when you can process them more fully. You can also do the breathing exercise and the senses exercise.

What's one thing you will do to take care of yourself today?

(5 min) Lead participants through this section.

Wrapping it up

What's one thing you want to remember from this lesson?

(1 min) Give participants time to complete "Wrapping it up." Assign the lament exercise as homework.

If you have 120 minutes, give extra time for discussing laments and sharing at end of the ceremony, or use content from "Looking Back" on p. 63–66.

Decide in advance how you will destroy the torn papers.

Voices

Lament of a Forgiven Son

Father you Created me, you Knew me Even when I was in my mothers womb. What a disappointment I must have been when you looked upon me, for from the beginning I suffered, from the moment I came into this world my life has been full of torment and pain. From my Fathers hand Death tried to seize me, pain and fear ruled my life til the age of fourteen—when truth from my mother's life set me free; Only to set me up for the next tramatic scene to Grip my Life, to riddle my hopes and Dreams, with agony and pain. Death to come in and take from me the only women I had and would ever Love, but not only my Queen but the child I longed to love, my "baby Girl" who I would never be able to hold-to-comfort in her time of fear—of a world filled with hatred and evil, to read to her and watch over her as she slept, to Laugh with her and when in pain, to cry with and shield her as best I could from all Evil. Which til this Day the pain and agony of there memory Cripples me. I am stuck in my mind of what could and should have been. So I Replace Love with addiction and pain. Until the Death at my birth catches up with me, to write the mistake of my Fathers hand. For truly I wish i had died that day.

For what good is man, but to be fruitful and multiply. I have no wife, no heir, nothing to remind the world that I existed. So Lord what truly Did my birth accomplish. Why my Lord? Why Let me Live? End the pain which is my life.

My Lord Creator of heaven and earth Look down and have mercy on me for the trouble of my heart is heavy. If you dont help me truly the weight shall crush me. for my tears dont stop flowing and I am weak from sobbing. I cant eat for food no longer sustains me. There is no pleasure no taste in my mouth. The water I drink just feeds the tears of my heart. Help me Lord for I am tired and there is no rest for me.

Father God from the day of my youth I was taught of your Love and mercy, how it endurers forever, and how your love is always present. So I Shall still my heart and trust in you, for I know you are my savior my God and my King. And that the whole world is under your Dominion. I know you are a just God and that you hear the cries of your people. So I shall wait on you my Lord. for I know true Deliverance comes from you.

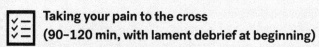

Taking your pain to the cross
(90–120 min, with lament debrief at beginning)

Before you begin, gather the following:
- paper for participants to write their pain on
- if possible, instrumental music for Section 1 and song sheets or recorded music for Section 2
- a brown paper bag to collect torn papers

Objectives:
By the end of this lesson we want to be able to:
- Identify our heart wounds and share them with another person.
- Understand that Christ died to bring us healing as well as forgiveness.
- Help others bring their pain to the cross of Christ.

TAKING YOUR PAIN TO THE CROSS

(20 min) Discuss the lament exercise. Invite participants to share, in small or large group, using the questions on p. 41.

(1 min) Introduce the lesson title and objectives.

Taking care of yourself

When we remember painful experiences, we need to stay aware of our bodies and to remind ourselves that we are no longer in the past. Consider using the breathing exercise or the senses exercise before starting this lesson.

(5 min) Lead participants through this section, using one of the exercises indicated.

Pain to the cross ceremony

We have taken time to recognize the pains we are carrying. We've expressed our pain by sharing and listening to one another, in laments, and in the art exercise. Now we will bring those pains to the cross where Jesus died and ask him to bring healing to our wounded hearts. We will do a ceremony where we write down the wounds of our hearts, then bring these wounds and pain to Jesus.

You may find this ceremony helpful. It will not necessarily heal all heart wounds instantaneously. You may need to bring your pain to Christ again many times in the healing process. You can do so in your thoughts and prayers, even in the middle of the night.

(1 min) Read these introductory paragraphs aloud, to give an overview of the ceremony.

1. Identify the wounds of your heart

We are here to take our pain to the cross. We are taught in Scripture that Jesus came not only to bear our sins but also to bear our pain and heal us. In the Gospel according to Matthew we read: *"When evening came, people brought to Jesus many who had demons in them. Jesus drove out the evil spirits with a word and healed all who were sick. He did this to make come true what the prophet Isaiah had said, 'He himself took our sickness and carried away our diseases'"* (Matthew 8:16–17).

Section 1 (37 min)

(2 min) Read aloud. If appropriate, invite some participants to read portions.

Matthew was quoting from the book of Isaiah, which says: "*We despised him and rejected him; he endured suffering and pain.... But he endured the suffering that should have been ours, the pain we should have borne. All the while we thought that his suffering was punishment sent by God*" (Isaiah 53:3–4).

In Luke 4 we learn that Jesus went to the synagogue and read aloud from the book of the prophet Isaiah: "*The Spirit of the Lord is upon me because he has chosen me to bring good news to the poor. He has sent me to proclaim liberty to the captives and recovery of sight to the blind, to set free the oppressed and announce that the time has come when the Lord will save his people*" (Luke 4:18–19).

We further learn that after reading this passage, "*Jesus rolled up the scroll, gave it to the attendant, and sat down. All the people in the synagogue had their eyes fixed on him as he said to them, 'This passage of scripture has come true today, as you heard it being read'*" (Luke 4:20–21).

Jesus felt the full burden of human pain and sinfulness. Jesus knows the pain that is in our hearts. We need to bring it to him so that he can heal us. In this exercise, we will bring our pain to the cross.

» Write down your worst pain

- Painful things that have been done to you.
- Painful things you have seen done to others, or bad dreams you have had.
- Painful things you have heard about that have happened to others.
- Painful things that you have done to others.

Write these things on another sheet of paper.

Share your pain.

 DISCUSSION

In small groups, share as much or as little as you wish of what you wrote down, or share what the process of writing it down was like. Listen without criticizing or offering advice. Share openly but don't dwell on violent parts. Pray for each other if you feel comfortable doing so.

(15 min) Read prompts, then give out paper. Encourage them to write those things that are most painful and that they don't like to think about. Mention the following:

- No one else will see their paper; the papers will be destroyed afterward.
- They will have about 15 minutes to write.
- Keep quiet once finished, to not disturb those who are still writing.

If possible, play non-distracting instrumental music quietly in the background.

(20 min) Small groups of two to three. Make sure no one is left out.

2. Bring your wounds and pain to Jesus

Isaiah 53:4–6 says:

> But he endured the suffering that should have been ours,
> the pain that we should have borne.
> All the while we thought that his suffering
> was punishment sent by God.
> But because of our sins he was wounded,
> beaten because of the evil we did.
> We are healed by the punishment he suffered,
> made whole by the blows he received.
> All of us were like sheep that were lost,
> each of us going his own way.
> But the Lord made the punishment fall on him,
> the punishment all of us deserved.

Talk to Jesus about your pain.

Take some time to bring your pain to Jesus. Tell him exactly what it is—anger, sadness, loneliness, feeling abandoned. Try to let out all the pain and emotions you feel about your loss or hurt.

Section 2 (20 min)

(3 min) Read aloud. If appropriate, invite a participant to read the verse. Give a few minutes of silence for participants to quietly talk to God.

(5 min)

• Invite participants to bring their pain to the cross.

• Have participants tear their paper into 5–6 pieces (it should be able to fit in their open hand).

• Have them clench their fist, as you say, "This is how you have hung onto your pain, not knowing what to do with it. Now we know what to do with it. We can bring it to the cross."

• Have them open their hand and turn it quickly over onto the cross, "nailing" their papers to the cross.

• As they do, they can say, "I'm handing over my suffering to Jesus, who died on the cross for me."

Bring your pain to the cross.

Say (out loud if possible), "I'm handing over my suffering to Jesus, who died on the cross for me."

48
Healing the Wounded Heart

Destroy the papers.

Isaiah 61:1–3 says:

> The Sovereign LORD has filled me with his Spirit.
> He has chosen me and sent me
> to bring good news to the poor,
> to heal the broken-hearted,
> to announce release to captives
> and freedom to those in prison.
> He has sent me to proclaim that the time has come
> when the Lord will save his people
> and defeat their enemies.
> He has sent me to comfort all who mourn,
> to give to those who mourn in Zion
> joy and gladness instead of grief,
> a song of praise instead of sorrow.
> They will be like trees
> that the LORD himself has planted.
> They will all do what is right,
> and God will be praised for what he has done.

(5 min)

• Have all the participants tear up their papers into the smallest pieces possible and place them into a brown paper bag.

• Explain how you will take them home and destroy them. (This is important to tell them.) If possible, take a picture or video as you do so, and show participants during the next session.

• Then read the verse; if appropriate, have a volunteer read it.

(2 min)

If appropriate, give a few minutes of silence for participants to pray for the other participants in the class, that God will heal all brokenness in their hearts.

(5 min)

If possible, play or sing a song such as "Amazing Grace/My Chains Are Gone" or "It Is Well with My Soul."

Time permitting, invite participants to share what God has done in them this week.

(5 min) Express in your own words. If appropriate, lead participants through one of the exercises suggested.

Taking care of yourself

Remembering the most painful things in your life takes a lot of courage and energy. It is normal to feel more tired or emotional than usual, or to have difficulty sleeping. Don't be discouraged. Recognize and celebrate the ways you have been courageous.

Remember the exercises you've learned to cope with strong emotions. Before you leave, consider doing the breathing exercise or the senses exercise.

What's one thing you will do to take care of yourself today?

_____

_____

_____

_____

(1 min) Give participants time to complete "Wrapping it up."

Wrapping it up

What's one thing you want to remember from this lesson?

_____

_____

_____

Voices

December 12, 2016

When I walked into the class room at Douglas County Corrections, at age 56, I was facing my (4) fourth prison number and a parole violation from my (3) third prison number.

The scars were so deeply hidden—I could not verbally express them

Struck down by physical abuse of the body, I thought it was no cure. My life was chaotic, and out of control. You feel ungodly when ungodly things happen to you. I was hurt—hopeless—it was too hard to move on.

I started stuffing instead of forgiving. I ran from one pain to find another.

Where is the comfort, and peace I once knew in God.

What is this pain thats holding me back from the blessed life I deserve to live. My emotions can not cope with the pain

The drugs could not numb the pain. The alcohol could not drown the pain. The abcess had made a hole so deep and ugly in my heart.

How could God heal me? Physically. Emotionally. Spiritually Exhausted.

How can the wounds of the heart heal

Walking in the class room—My God gave me the strength to talk about the trauma (the core of my pain).

I talked—I cried, I grieved, got mad

I called on God, and shared my complaints. I asked for help, and trusted in His Power. The soothing oil from Jesus poured over me, as I nailed my pain to the cross.

I have seen my own brokeness, and given every shattered piece to God. Through His grace and mercy—Praise honor and glory belong to Him. God snatched me out—before I fell in deep depression

He knows me better than anyone. I don't have to keep exhausting myself trying to rebuild my life after another shipwreck.

He controls the storm.

Through his grace and mercy I see a new vision. I see the others, the 97% of women who suffer trauma, and don't know it.

Now I have an eye to see the other's and extend a helping hand.

The grace to step outside myself.

Real and fake forgiveness skits

(Have participants use their own names)

Skit 1. There is nothing to forgive
(3 participants)

Tim is sitting with his friend, Bruce. He says, "Last week Samuel really hurt me. Right in front of all the other church leaders he said I was no good at preaching. I can't get over it. It still hurts when I think about it." After Bruce leaves, Samuel walks in. Samuel says, "Please forgive me for what I said last week." Then Tim says, "There is nothing to forgive. I didn't mind."

Skit 2. Until you forget, you haven't forgiven
(2 participants)

Pastor Jackson is talking to Nate, a church member. Nate says, "I've tried to forgive my father for being cruel to me when I was a child, but it is hard." Pastor Jackson says, "Well you must forget all about that. Until you forget, you can't say you have forgiven him."

Skit 3. I forgive you for the hurt you caused me
(2–3 participants)

Lamont taught the adult Bible class last Sunday in the place of the regular teacher. A member of the class, Silas, argued a lot about a minor point Lamont taught. Later that week, when the regular teacher thanked him, Lamont said, "I never want to teach that class again!" He explained what had happened and how Silas had embarrassed him. The teacher offered to go with him to discuss it all with Silas.

When they got to Silas's house, Lamont expressed his dismay at the argument in class, his frustration at not being able to answer well enough, and his embarrassment. Silas apologized and asked his forgiveness, which Lamont was eager to give.

How can we forgive others? (90 min)

This lesson intended to be followed by "Looking back" (p. 63–66), which takes 30 minutes.

Before you begin:

- Rehearse the real and fake forgiveness skits.
- Prepare slips of paper with the verse references you will use on p. 54–55.
- Rehearse the locked-arms skit.

Objectives

By the end of this lesson we want to be able to:

- Define real forgiveness versus fake forgiveness.
- Explain how and why we need to forgive others.
- Describe the process of true repentance.
- Identify those we need to forgive or ask forgiveness from.

HOW CAN WE FORGIVE OTHERS?

Taking care of yourself

There are things we can do when we're not stressed, to help ourselves cope when we are stressed. It's like packing for a road trip—you don't need things now, but you will need them later. If you have time, try the tree exercise on page 65.

1. Forgiveness skits

Think about the forgiveness skits you saw or participated in. (1) "There is nothing to forgive." (2) "Until you forget, you haven't forgiven." (3) "I forgive you for the hurt you caused me."

 DISCUSSION

1. Which of these situations show real forgiveness?

2. How is it different from the others?

2. Forgiveness is not ...

Forgiveness is not	Forgiveness is

(3 min) Check in with participants to see how they're feeling after the intensity of previous lesson. Tell them how you destroyed the papers. If applicable, show them the picture or video you took.

(1 min) Introduce the lesson title and objectives.

(1 min) Paraphrase this section. Guide participants through the tree exercise, or wait to do it at the end of the class, during "Looking Back."

Section 1 (10 min)

(5 min) Skits. Have participants do the three real and fake forgiveness skits (see opposite page).

(5 min) Large group. Discuss these two questions.

Section 2 (15 min)

(5 min) Small group. Using skits as background, have half the groups discuss what forgiveness is not, and the other half discuss what forgiveness is.

(10 min) Large group. Get feedback. List responses on board/flip chart. Top up "forgiveness is not" column with content on p. 54. (The next section focuses on what forgiveness is.)

Forgiveness is not ...

- Saying the offense didn't matter or that we were not hurt by what the person did.
- Being able to make sense of why the person did what he or she did.
- Acting as if the event never happened.
- Dependent on the offender apologizing first or changing their behavior.
- Letting those who do wrong avoid the consequences of their action.
- Letting the offender hurt us or other innocent people again.
- Trusting a person again right after they hurt us.

Section 3 (20 min)

(10 min) Say, "Let's talk more about what forgiveness is, and how we can do it." Express this content in your own words. Have participants read as many verse references as time permits.

3. How can we forgive others?

If we think forgiving is too hard for us to do, we are right. God is the only one who can enable us to forgive (1 Peter 2:24).

Bring the pain to Christ.

Forgiving someone begins when we recognize that the person has wronged us and we accept the pain their sin has caused us. To say it has not hurt if it did is to lie, and we are called to speak the truth (Ephesians 4:25). We bring our pain to the cross and release it to Jesus. When Jesus heals our pain, then we will be able to forgive those who have hurt us.

Do not wait for the other person to apologize.

Often we are unwilling to forgive until the offender has apologized to us. Or we want to see that the person has changed their behavior before we forgive them. Like Jesus, we need to forgive people, even if they are not sorry about the evil they have done (Romans 5:8). On the cross he said, "Forgive them, Father! They don't know what they are doing" (Luke 23:34).

Allow time for the process.

Offense

Complete
Forgiveness

When we forgive someone, we will still remember what happened. At first, we may still feel the pain associated with it. When this happens, we need to continue to take the parts that hurt to Jesus. The commitment to forgive often comes before the feelings of forgiveness, and sometimes long before. As we bring our hurt to Jesus over and over, eventually we will feel less pain when we remember the event.

Let wrongdoers face the consequences of their actions.

Forgiving someone does not mean that they will not be punished if they have done wrong things. By forgiving, we allow God to judge and take revenge (Romans 12:19).

God uses the authorities to deal with those who break the law (Romans 13:1–4). Even though we have forgiven someone, it may be necessary to bring them to justice to prevent others from being hurt in the future. Forgiveness does not mean the offender is excused from paying back what was taken (Numbers 5:5–7).

 DISCUSSION

What are some common sayings about forgiveness in our society? How do they compare with what the Bible tells us?

Draw picture on board/flip chart. Explain that forgiveness does not happen all at once.

- We start to forgive, but sometimes we circle back as we remember the hurt of the offense.
- Then we forgive again a little more thoroughly.
- Gradually we make our way to complete forgiveness.
- Sometimes the first step is asking God to help you *want* to forgive.

(10 min) **Small group**, then **large group** feedback.

Section 4 (20 min)

(5 min) Mention section title. Do the "Locked-arms skit" (see below) to illustrate why God wants us to forgive others. Bring out that when we don't forgive, we are the ones who suffer.

(5 min) Small group. Have each group discuss one of the verses in this section and tell what it says about why we should forgive.

(5 min) Large group. Get feedback. Top up with content on opposite page.

Locked-arms skit

Get a volunteer of the same gender as you. Explain that you have been offended by your friend (the volunteer), and then lock arms with the volunteer, standing back to back.

Say: Everywhere I go, I drag my friend with me like a dead weight. This is exhausting and frustrating for me.

Now say (while acting out the actions described):

- When I take a walk, my friend is there.
- When I eat supper, my friend is there.
- When I try to do my work, my friend is there.
- When I pray, my friend is there.
- When I try to run away, my friend follows.
- When I try to hide, my friend is right there.

F56

4. Why does God want us to forgive other people?

Consider the following verses:

- Ephesians 4:26–27
- 2 Corinthians 2:10–11
- Hebrews 12:14–15
- 1 John 4:10
- Ephesians 4:32
- Matthew 18:21–35

- No matter where I go I cannot escape my thoughts and feelings about my friend. I cannot escape them until I forgive.

Now say, "I forgive you" and, as you do, unlock arms.

Say: Forgiveness is a gift that we have received from God, and one that we should also pass along to others (Matthew 18:22–35).

Forgiveness frees us from anger and bitterness.

- When we are angry, we can give Satan a foothold in our hearts (Ephesians 4:26-27).
- Refusing to forgive can make us physically ill. It may make us become as violent and evil as those who offended us. Forgiveness releases us from all this. We forgive for our own good (2 Corinthians 2:10-11).
- If we do not forgive others, we pass our hatred on to our children, resulting in cycles of revenge and violence between groups which can go on for generations, poisoning people (Hebrews 12:14-15).

Forgiveness shows that we understand Christ's sacrifice and our salvation.

- When we understand how much we have offended God by our sinfulness, and how Jesus offered himself for our forgiveness even before we repented (1 John 4:10), any offense we have experienced will seem small.
- We will want to extend that same forgiveness to others (Ephesians 4:32; Matthew 18:21-35).

Forgiveness allows us to be reconciled with those who have offended us.

- Until we forgive those who have offended us, our relationship with them will suffer.
- Forgiveness makes it possible for our relationship with them to be restored.
- Full restoration, however, requires repentance and forgiveness by both parties.

Forgiveness can sometimes change the person who offended us.

- Forgiving someone may be the start of God bringing that person to repentance.
- In Acts 7, as Stephen was dying, he forgave those who were killing him. One of those people was Saul, who later became Paul the apostle (Acts 7:59—8:1).

DISCUSSION, IN SMALL GROUPS

1. What do you find the hardest thing about forgiving someone?

2. What has helped you the most to forgive others?

(5 min) Small group. No large group feedback, as this is a personal discussion.

(5 min) Mention section title, then ask "How can we repent?" Paraphrase this content. Consider having participants read some of the verses.

(15 min) Read through the exercise with participants, then give them time to reflect and fill it out.

5. What if we are the ones who have caused the offense?

We need to repent ...

- Allow God's Spirit to show us how much our sin hurts God and others (James 4:8-9; 2 Corinthians 7:10).
- Take responsibility for what we have done and clearly state our sin (Proverbs 28:13; Psalm 32:3-5).
- Seek God's forgiveness of our sin, and then accept that God has done so (1 John 1:9).
- Ask those we've offended to forgive us, without excusing ourselves, blaming them, or demanding that they trust us again right away (James 5:16).
- Show our repentance by the way we act (Acts 26:20b).
- If possible, pay back what was taken (Numbers 5:5-7).

» *Forgiveness exercise*

If you need to forgive someone:

Write down the name of a person (or people) you need to forgive. Use a symbol to represent the person if you are concerned about privacy:

_____

What do you need to forgive them for?

How did their actions make you feel?

Pray: "God, I forgive *[or, please help me to forgive]* _____
for doing _____ .

It made me feel _____."

If you need to be forgiven for harm you have done:

I need to ask _____ to forgive me.

What harm did you do to them?

How might you have made them feel?

Pray: "God, please forgive me for doing _____
to _____ . Please help me do the things
that show I have repented."

What plans can you make to ask the person you hurt for forgiveness?

If we confess our sins to God, he will keep his promise and do what is right: he will forgive us our sins and purify us from all our wrongdoing.
(1 John 1:9)

(5 min) Lead participants through this section. If needed, do one of the suggested exercises.

Taking care of yourself

Take a moment to see how you are feeling now. Do you need to do a breathing exercise or the senses exercise? What's one thing you can do to take care of yourself today?

_____

_____

_____

_____

(1 min) Give participants time to complete "Wrapping it up."

Wrapping it up

What's one thing you want to remember from this lesson?

_____

_____

_____

_____

_____

Voices

Things started off rough in my life from the very beginning. My dad was a violent alcoholic and my older brother and I witnessed a lot of abuse with my father beating my mother. When my mother was pregnant with me, my dad held my brother and mother hostage at gun point. Violence was a constant occurrence in our home until age four, when they finally divorced. Our lives became normal enough after that. I lived with my mom and I got a good step dad. I had friends and we played Barbie; I liked sports. Our family went together to the Catholic Church. Things became pretty normal.

My brother, however, always seemed to be in trouble and my parent's full attention was on him. Like my dad, he was very violent not only to family members but would tear up the house in his rages. They were always correcting and disciplining him until finally one day, they gave him over to the state. I think this is when I remember the shift happening in our family. I felt a sense of uneasiness that my parents would give up on him. I got the feeling that if I did enough wrong, they would give me up as well. Also at this time with my brother gone, all of their attentions turned in my direction. That correction and discipline they had used on my brother was suddenly focused on me. From the age of 10 to age 18 my mom, with the help of my step dad, would hold me down and spank me like a little child when I did wrong. I felt humiliation with this and really hated being restrained by my step dad. I began seething with anger.

I had always done well in school. I was a good student, a cheerleader, and even received a college scholarship in cheerleading, and I was active in sports. I did, however, still have a huge amount of anger built up inside of me. I learned to release it by fighting. Usually on a weekly basis, matches would be arranged in a field for me and a large number of kids from our small town, 60 to 80, would gather to watch me fight. This was the only way I knew how to release my building, internal rage.

One time when I was about 15, my mother drug tested me and discovered that I tested positive for pot. To punish me my step-dad held me down so my mom could spank me. He had on a robe and I could feel his unclothed body under the robe up against my skin. I was screaming for him to get off me but he kept holding me down. Out of desperation I bit him. My parents' response was to call the police and let me sit in jail for five days. They then kicked me out of the house. I ended up losing all my scholarships for college as I scrambled to live life on my own. It was at this time that I started using cocaine, alcohol, and eventually crack.

During the process of all of this chaos, I had two beautiful children. Sadly, I raised them with this explosive anger and they experienced many things children should not see.

I was arrested in March 2016 on an assault charge. The night before I was arrested I had been in a fight with my boyfriend and threw my cell phone at him so hard that I cracked his skull. While in jail I caught an additional assault on a woman who I had cut with a knife and brutally beat. I was in once again in jail full of anger, hatred, and rage. I was like a bomb ready to explode.

It was during my jail stay that I heard about this class on trauma healing. I was asked to sign up. I not only came to faith in Christ during this class but God brought this entire trauma in my life to the forefront. I had no idea that the trauma of my childhood was the underlying factor in my anger. It was always under the surface ready to explode but the class taught me how to deal with it. I was taught how to deal with it by writing laments, talking, and bringing it to the cross and eventually forgiveness. I know now that if I did not let God heal the trauma, I would be back in jail on another assault charge.

When I first came to jail, I was often locked down for fighting. That was who I was. But after taking the class and getting to the root of my anger, I have since walked away from countless encounters. One day the chaplain who taught the trauma class was in the housing unit and was able to witness first hand the change that has taken place in my life. I had an inmate try to verbally provoke a physical fight with me. She was in my face, being physically aggressive, screaming obscenities. Oh, my old behavior would have unleashed on this woman but I was able to put both my hands in the air, walk away, and go to my cell. The women even followed after me with taunts but I no longer felt the need to fight.

I see so many women in jail come in and out and in again whose hearts are overflowing with pain. There are so many who have unresolved trauma in their lives. My desire is to first go back to be a loving mom with my kids in Colorado but eventually go into the jail and conduct trauma healing classes. These classes have truly changed my life.

**Looking back
(25 min)**

This session can be added to the end of the forgiveness lesson, or done as a stand-alone lesson to conclude the healing group.

LOOKING BACK

In this final section you will find three ways of thinking about your life and your struggles that may help you see your life story differently. You'll also find an exercise to help you take care of yourself on the journey.

1. How does God use suffering?

 DISCUSSION

1. How has God used suffering in your life?
2. Read the following verses and discuss how God has used suffering in people's lives:

    •   1 Peter 1:6–7
    •   Genesis 50:18–20
    •   Isaiah 40:11
    •   2 Corinthians 1:3–5.

(1 min) Express this content in your own words.

(1 min) Introduce as follows:
• Evil is evil, but there's nothing God can't redeem. He will always get the last word.
• We can't explain why God allows us to suffer. Even if we could, it would not take away the pain.
• It can be helpful to look back on our lives to see how God has used our suffering in ways that have resulted in at least some good.

(8 min) Discuss Question 1 in pairs. Tell participants when half the time has passed, so they can switch who is speaking.

(7 min) Discussion Q. 2, large group. Top up with:

• God uses suffering to purify our faith (1 Peter 1:6–7).
• God turns evil into good (Genesis 50:18–20).
• God comforts us in our suffering so we can comfort others (Isaiah 40:11; 2 Corinthians 1:3–5).

(3 min) Express this content in your own words. Draw the diagram on board/flip chart if needed.

2. The healing journey

Take another look at the healing journey diagram. We have learned several steps of the process of healing from heart wounds—expressing our pain through words and art, grieving, lamenting, bringing our pain to the cross, and forgiving. As we continue to practice these steps, we will be able to rebuild our lives and be better able to face suffering in the future. We will have good days and bad days—it's all part of the journey. And as we learned in this group, we can talk to God at every step.

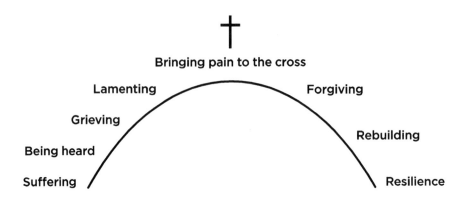

Taking care of yourself

This exercise can help us build the ability to handle tough situations and emotions and prepare our mind for future conflict.

» Tree exercise

Read Psalm 1:1–3a.

> Happy are those who reject the advice of evil people,
> who do not follow the example of sinners
> or join those who have no use for God.
>
> Instead, they find joy in obeying the Law of the LORD,
> and they study it day and night.
>
> They are like trees that grow beside a stream,
> that bear fruit at the right time,
> and whose leaves do not dry up.

Now fix your eyes in one place or, if you're comfortable, close your eyes. Imagine that you are a tree.

- What kind of tree would you be? See yourself as that kind of tree.
- In your imagination, look around. Is your tree by itself?
- What's the landscape around you?

Now look at the trunk of the tree.

- Notice it going down into the earth and up into the branches. Follow the branches way out into the leaves. (If it's a fruit tree, see the fruit hanging from the branches.)

Now follow the trunk down to the roots.

- Look at the roots—is it a long single root or many roots going out? Notice how the roots are anchored into the ground.
- Now watch how the root system is bringing water and nutrients to the roots and how those nutrients travel up the tree to the branches.

(5 min) Present this content, then lead participants through the tree exercise. As you conclude the session, direct participants' attention to the "On Your Own" section (p. 67 and following).

Notice the weather.

- Imagine the sun shining on the leaves, making oxygen. Imagine the tree just being there in just the right temperature and light.
- Now the tree needs a bit of water. Imagine a gentle rain slowly coming down over the leaves and going towards the roots. See the water going down, down into the roots. See the moisture being taken up into the tree.
- Now stop the rain; see the sun coming out to dry the leaves.

Now imagine the tree with some live creatures—perhaps birds, or squirrels or insects going up and down. Watch all the activity.

Now there's a storm.

- Black clouds are beginning to form in the distance. The storm won't harm or destroy the tree but the storm will come.
- The wind is picking up and the clouds are coming. The branches are shaking. The trunk is moving back and forth. Some of the leaves are falling and some of the fruit is falling.
- Now focus on how the roots are holding firm and allowing the tree to move back and forth in the wind. Let the storm go on a bit. Feel the tree moving back and forth with its roots firmly planted in the ground.
- Now the storm is slowing gradually until everything is still again.
- How is the tree feeling after the storm?
- Now the sun is returning. The insects and birds are coming back out again.
- Things are drying. Imagine the tree coming back to normal.
- When the tree is still again, the sun is shining, and the insects and the birds are back out again, gradually take some deep breaths and open your eyes.

ON YOUR OWN

The final pages of this journal are for you. Do you have a story of healing? Do you have something you want to share with God?

_____
_____
_____
_____
_____
_____
_____
_____
_____
_____
_____
_____
_____
_____
_____
_____
_____
_____
_____
_____

PREPARING TO LEAD YOUR OWN HEALING GROUPS

INTRODUCTION

Program overview

This handbook is for facilitators to assist hurting people using *Healing the Wounded Heart: An Inmate Journal*. It is adapted from *Healing the Wounds of Trauma: How the Church Can Help*, the classic Bible-based trauma healing program for adults.

This diagram summarizes the process of trauma healing as experienced by participants:

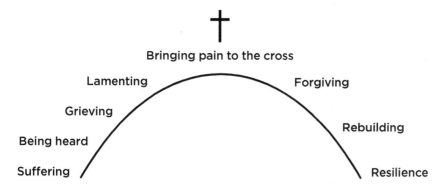

When people experience suffering and loss, their hearts can be wounded. For these wounds to heal, people need to express their pain to someone who listens to them without causing further harm. They need to accept the pain of the loss and grieve so that those feelings are not buried alive inside them. They can express these feelings honestly to God in lament. Once identified and expressed, they can bring that pain to Christ, who died on the cross for sin and everything sin brought with it: death, pain, sickness, conflict, abuse, and so forth. As we experience Christ's healing, we come to a place where we can begin to forgive those who have hurt us. We can begin to rebuild our lives and communities. We are better able to face suffering in the future.

Program model

The Trauma Healing Institute program model usually uses the following stages:

- **Convening Session:** To help top leaders experience and understand the trauma healing program, and decide if they want it.
- **Equipping Session:** To train people to lead healing groups. This is done through a three-step process: an initial training, a practicum (leading two healing groups), and an advanced training. Some will be selected to lead trainings (see "Becoming a trauma healing facilitator" on page F71).

- **Healing Group:** The goal is to help people with heart wounds to find healing, engage with Scripture, and become more resilient. Healing groups cover at least the five core lessons.
- **Trauma Healing Mini:** To address trauma related to a specific need, but without covering the five core lessons.
- **Community of Practice:** The network of facilitators using these materials. At times they gather for networking, collaboration, professional development, encouragement, and prayer, and may invite mental health professionals and leaders from organizations and churches that work with trauma survivors.

Program materials

Trauma healing materials are available for different audiences and purposes:

 (Initial model)

- *Healing the Wounds of Trauma: How the Church Can Help* (American Bible Society, 2013; expanded edition, 2016). The classic program's core book for adults. The *Classic Program Facilitator Handbook* provides additional help for leading sessions. (The first half of the full handbook is published separately as the *Starter Handbook*.)
- *Healing the Wounded Heart: An Inmate Journal*, an adaptation of the above materials for correctional facilities, along with a facilitator's guide.
- *Scripture Companion Booklet*: For those who are in a healing group but do not have a Bible, or for new readers who find a booklet easier to read than a Bible. This booklet contains the main ideas of each lesson and Scripture passages written out in full. Healing group participants can review what they have learned and meditate on the Scripture passages.
- *Healing Hearts Club Story and Activity Book* and *Healing Children's Wounds of Trauma: Facilitator Book*. Trauma healing for children 8–13. The same ideas as in *Healing the Wounds of Trauma*, but communicated by means of stories, games, exercises, crafts, and activities.
- *Story-based Trauma Healing:* For use by live storytellers. The same ideas as *Healing the Wounds of Trauma*, communicated by means of Bible stories, current life stories, exercises, and memory verses put to song. Literacy is not required for facilitators or healing group members. A Story Book with discussion guide is available, as well as a facilitator handbook.
- *Audio Trauma Healing.* Professionally produced audio dramas with small group discussion and Scripture songs, for broadcasting on radio or other devices.
- *Online Database*: The trauma healing database records information on facilitators, program activities, and translations. Facilitators and administrators can request a log-in by sending an e-mail to **traumahealing@americanbible.org.**
- *Materials Development Handbook:* Gives information on contextualizing the materials, translation, and licensing.

Trauma healing publications are available at your local Bible Society or through **traumahealinginstitute.org.**

discount - ABS2S

BECOMING A TRAUMA HEALING FACILITATOR

■ = certification

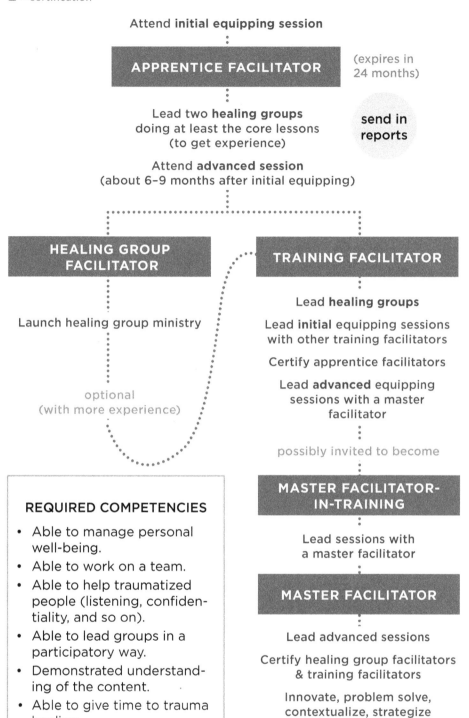

Attend **initial equipping session**

APPRENTICE FACILITATOR

(expires in 24 months)

Lead two **healing groups**
doing at least the core lessons
(to get experience)

send in reports

Attend **advanced session**
(about 6–9 months after initial equipping)

HEALING GROUP FACILITATOR

TRAINING FACILITATOR

Launch healing group ministry

optional
(with more experience)

Lead **healing groups**

Lead **initial** equipping sessions
with other training facilitators

Certify apprentice facilitators

Lead **advanced** equipping
sessions with a master
facilitator

possibly invited to become

MASTER FACILITATOR-IN-TRAINING

Lead sessions with
a master facilitator

MASTER FACILITATOR

Lead advanced sessions

Certify healing group facilitators
& training facilitators

Innovate, problem solve,
contextualize, strategize

REQUIRED COMPETENCIES

- Able to manage personal well-being.
- Able to work on a team.
- Able to help traumatized people (listening, confidentiality, and so on).
- Able to lead groups in a participatory way.
- Demonstrated understanding of the content.
- Able to give time to trauma healing.

FACILITATING GROUPS

Facilitating groups well requires three things: participatory learning, using visual aids well, and managing group dynamics.

Participatory learning

Participatory learning is an essential part of the trauma healing process. It is more effective than traditional teaching methods, because people remember:

- 20 percent of what they hear
- 30 percent of what they see
- 70 percent of what they discuss with others
- 80 percent of what they experience
- 95 percent of what they teach others

Participatory learning is also a critical part of the healing process because it gives people the opportunity to interact and tell their stories.

If you say less, the participants will learn more. Participatory learning respects the knowledge and experience the group brings and allows people to interact personally with the ideas. Engaging the mind, emotions, and body all together makes for the best learning experience. Laughter also helps people learn. The more creative, the better—and people can be surprisingly creative.

"None of us is as smart as all of us."

Take the temperature of the group and adjust to keep energy flowing. Participatory learning means you give up some control as the leader and take risks, because you can't predict what people will say. The risks are well worth it!

Look for the teachable moment: People may ask questions about something you plan to cover later. This is a teachable moment. Flex and deal with the question. You can throw it back to the group first and then add your own thoughts as necessary. People can also ask questions that are not related to the topic of the lesson. If they are topics that should be discussed, designate a flip chart paper or part of the board as a "refrigerator" where questions can be stored for a later time. Be sure to find a time to respond to these!

Create a safe space: Don't force people to share, or shame them by disagreeing with them publicly.

Discuss confidentiality (page F6). Use name tent cards or name tags.

Planning a lesson: Think first of how you will have the group participate, not what you will present. Say just enough to introduce the topic and ask discussion questions (or give instructions for an exercise). These questions (or instructions) need to be very clear and contribute to the direction of the lesson. The questions in the book have been carefully crafted. If you decide to use other questions, test them first.

After the group participation, always get some feedback to find out what the group already knows. Add anything from the book not already stated. Then transition to the next section of the lesson. See the diagram on page F73.

THE BASIC MODEL FOR PARTICIPATORY LEARNING

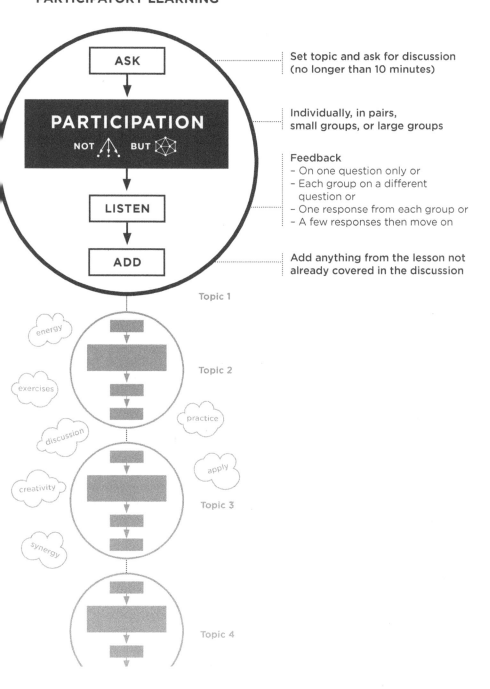

ASK
Set topic and ask for discussion
(no longer than 10 minutes)

PARTICIPATION
NOT △ BUT ◇
Individually, in pairs,
small groups, or large groups

Feedback
- On one question only or
- Each group on a different
  question or
- One response from each group or
- A few responses then move on

LISTEN

ADD
Add anything from the lesson not
already covered in the discussion

Topic 1
Topic 2
Topic 3
Topic 4

energy
exercises
discussion
creativity
synergy
practice
apply

As much as possible, have the participants **practice** new skills—for example, the listening exercise, writing a lament, writing a letter to a loved one who has committed suicide, and so forth.

Allow time for them to **apply** what they have learned to their lives. There are opportunities for this throughout the lessons.

Time management is an art. Be realistic about how much you can do in the time allotted. Guide the group without giving the impression that you don't have enough time. There is no need to say things like "We're short on time so we'll skip that." Just skip those parts without comment. Less is more: don't go into lecture mode. Keep it participatory and skip some of the content.

Using visual aids well

Visual aids can be anything from writing on a flip chart to objects that help people remember what has been said.

When writing on flip charts/white boards:

- Only write the important things. If you write everything, what's important will no longer stand out. It also gets monotonous. Less is more.
- Write clearly and large enough so people can read it. People don't benefit if they can't tell what is written.
- Stand to one side of what you're writing so people can see it.
- The discussion is the main activity. The writing should support the discussion, not steal the focus.
- If you have someone act as scribe for you, allow time for the scribe to write before moving on.

Trauma healing is participatory and every group is different. We discourage the use of computer-driven presentations using PowerPoint because they can keep you from responding to the unique dynamics of the group.

Managing group dynamics

The following table offers a list of problems that can arise in a group, along with ideas on how to deal with them.

Problem behaviors	Possible solutions
Talker: This person dominates groups by talking all the time.	"Let's hear from someone else now." Sometimes people like this are not aware that they are dominating, and you may need to talk to them privately.
Quiet: This person says nothing at all.	"What do you think about this question?" Don't force a quiet person to share if they don't want to, but do try to make a space for them to do so if they wish.
Off-topic: This person can take any subject off course, in a different direction than the facilitator wishes.	Reel the conversation back in. Guide the group back to the question on the table. Use the "refrigerator" as necessary (see page F72).
Misinformed: This person gives wrong information.	Ask the group if anyone else would like to comment. Let the group correct itself, if possible, but do not let wrong ideas go uncorrected.
Overwhelmed: This person erupts in sobbing and tears, unable to contain emotions.	Find someone who can go with the person to a quiet place where they can talk.

Problem behaviors	Possible solutions
Overwhelming: Someone may tell their story in such a graphic way it traumatizes others.	Before sharing begins, orient people to share their stories, but not to dwell on horrific parts as this may be upsetting to others.
Spiritual fixers: No matter the problem, this person has a Bible verse and advice. They minimize the pain of others, or try to fix everyone rather than listen.	Before the sharing begins, make it clear that the group is there to listen, not to fix or solve problems.
Offensive: Someone may be culturally inappropriate or disrespectful of other faith traditions.	Ensure that no one is marginalized. You may need to challenge someone privately for the good of the group.

PRACTICE FACILITATION EXERCISE

The practice facilitation exercise allows you to get experience facilitating in a safe environment and with feedback from others.

To prepare for the practice facilitation exercise, in small groups, select a section of the book that you have already covered in the training (excluding Pain to the Cross), and that you can present in ten minutes. Each person in your group should select a different section. Do not select the stories at the beginnings of the lessons. Assume that the group knows the story.

During your ten minutes, you will need to (1) present the topic and ask a question; (2) allow the group to participate and interact with each other; (3) listen to feedback from the group; and (4) add anything they have not covered. Use the diagram at right to structure your ten-minute session.

> **PRACTICE FACILITATION EXERCISE**
>
> (10 MIN TOTAL)
>
> Suggested breakdown:
> **Ask** (2 min)
> **Participation** (3 min)
> **Listen** (3 min)
> **Add** (2 min)

The following sections from the book are good for this amount of time:

* When we are suffering, what do we need to remember about God's character? (p. 10)
* What is a wound of the heart? (p. 22–23)
* How can we grieve in a way that brings healing? (p. 36–37)
* What forgiveness is not (p. 53–54)

Your facilitating skills will be assessed on a scale from 1–10, with 10 as excellent.

* *Very Good* (10–9 points): Communicates material from the book very clearly and accurately. Group participation organized very well. Responds very well to questions. Keeps the group functioning well. An enjoyable learning experience.
* *Good* (8–7 points): Communicates material from the book clearly and accurately. Group participation organized well. Responds well to questions. Some small issues in managing the group.
* *Fair* (6–5 points): Communicates material from the book accurately. Some group participation. Presentation or group participation not always well-planned or clear. Has some difficulty responding to questions and managing the group.
* *Weak* (4–3 points) Either preaches or lectures with very little or no group participation, or the presentation is confusing or inaccurate or focuses on material not in the book. Does not respond satisfactorily to questions. Not able to manage the group.
* *Very Weak* (2–1 point): Unable to communicate in a group. Unable to manage a group.

HEALING GROUP LOGISTICS

Getting authorization

Before you begin your healing group ministry, you need to get authorization from the appropriate leaders in your facility. The program overview brochures on the Trauma Healing Institute website may be helpful as you explain the program (see trauma-healinginstitute.org).

Recruiting

Then hold a recruiting session to explain the program to potential participants and to distribute a sign-up sheet (see page F83 for sample content).

Preparing

It is ideal for facilitators to work in teams of two, so they can balance each other's strengths and weaknesses.

The ideal number of participants in a healing group varies, but 6–12 works well. If it gets bigger than this, it becomes harder for everyone to participate. Participants do not necessarily need to share the same kind of trauma to form a healing group. The effects of trauma and paths of healing are similar regardless of the source of the trauma.

The lessons in this guide take about two hours each to complete. If you have less time, discuss with your mentor how you can modify them.

Some participants appreciate receiving a certificate of completion at the end of the class. See page F85 for a sample.

Reporting

After you finish your healing group, you will fill out a report and send it to your mentor, who will give you feedback. Your mentor will submit it to the Trauma Healing Institute (THI).

These reports are vital to the work of trauma healing because they:

1. tell THI which facilitators are active in which locations. This is especially important when THI receives requests from people needing trauma healing.

2. show THI financial partners how their investments are producing fruit.

3. encourage future financial partners, thus ensuring that the program can reach more traumatized people.

4. inform and expand the local community of practice.

Below is the official THI healing group report (available in electronic format on the facilitator's website, **traumahealinginstitute.org/facilitators**, under Reports).

Healing Group Report

Location City, State, Country		Main facilitator(s)	
Host organization		Assistant facilitator(s)	
Begin date		Lessons taught	☐ ALL ☐ Core lessons ☐ 1 ☐ 2 ☐ 3 ☐ 4 ☐ 5 ☐ 6 ☐ 6A ☐ 6B ☐ 6C ☐ 7 ☐ 8 ☐ 9 ☐ 10 ☐ 11 ☐ 11A
End date			
Times and duration of meeting (1x per wk for 2 hr, all day Sat, etc.)		Number who started	
Total number of hours the class met		Number who completed	
Primary language of sessions		Number who completed who are	_____ male _____ female
Other languages used		Number of participants who completed who are	_____ Anglican _____ Catholic _____ Orthodox _____ Protestant _____ Other: _____

What successes did you experience?

What challenges did you face?

Please provide at least two testimonies, with photos and authorization if possible.

Note: "Lessons taught" on the report reflects the lesson numbers of the Classic materials, which differ from the inmate journal. Here is the numbering for the lessons in the Classic materials:

- **Lesson 1: *If God loves us, why do we suffer?***
- **Lesson 2: *How can the wounds of our hearts be healed?***
- **Lesson 3: *What happens when someone is grieving?***
- Lesson 4: *Helping children who have experienced bad things*
- Lesson 5: *Helping someone who has been raped*
- Lesson 6: *Ministering amidst HIV & AIDS*
- Lesson 6A: *Domestic abuse*
- Lesson 6B: *Suicide*
- Lesson 6C: *Addictions*
- Lesson 7: *Care for the caregiver*
- **Lesson 8: *Taking your pain to the cross***
- **Lesson 9: *How can we forgive others?***
- Lesson 10: *Living as Christians in the midst of conflict*
- Lesson 11: *Preparing for trouble*
- Lesson 11A: *Helping people immediately after a disaster*

The bold font indicates the five "core lessons," which are included in the inmate journal. Check this box on the healing group report form if you complete these lessons in your healing group.

Try to fill out the report form on the previous page, using the following scenario:

> Chaplain Jones is ready to start a healing group in Housing Unit 12 at his large county jail in Atlanta. His co-leader is Bob Mission, a long-time and trusted volunteer. He has talked with Administrators and Programs and has received authorization to hold class once a month in Multipurpose 2, from 12:30 until 2:30, for five days in a row. He has been assigned the second Monday through Friday of each month, starting Monday, January 8.
>
> After the sign up of 12 male inmates, the first class had all in attendance. All spoke English except one inmate was primarily Spanish speaking but understood English. By the second class, two men were transferred to another housing unit so they had to drop the group. On the fourth day, one of the men had a surprise court date, got sentenced to 20 years State Prison and was too depressed to finish class so he also dropped. The class finished well and certificates of completion were given to all who completed the healing group.

Testimonies

If a participant has experienced healing through the healing group, writing and sharing their testimony can be a further step in their healing journey. Testimonies can bring glory to God and can also encourage people who are supporting your ministry. If you would like to share people's testimonies with others, ask them if they are willing to have their story shared. Never coerce them. If they're willing to share, have them sign the individual authorization form (see page F87). If you write the story for them, let them review the story before you share it with others and withdraw authorization if they wish. Their well-being is the first concern.

A testimony should include three parts:

1. the person and the problem (give details)
2. the trauma healing input that took place (give details)
3. how the person changed (give details)

Also be sure to get permission for photos. Use the individual and/or group authorization form as needed (both on page F87).

Healing group checklist

See the Healing Group Checklist starting on page F88 for a high-level checklist of facilitator responsibilities before, during, and after a healing group.

ORIENTATION TO CLASSIC TRAUMA HEALING MATERIALS

See page F90 for a description of the relationship between this Inmate edition of the trauma healing program and the original adult "Classic" edition.

WEBSITE

At TraumaHealingInstitute.org, you can access information on Trauma Healing worldwide, including upcoming events, promotional videos and brochures in English, French, and Spanish, and more. A password-protected part of the site has additional materials available for facilitators. Your trainer will request access to this part of the site for you. Record your user name and password here:

User name: _____

Password: _____

NEXT STEPS

1. Talk to the chaplain team in your jurisdiction about your plan to implement trauma healing at the jail/prison.

2. Talk to the administration at your facility about the feasibility of implementing the program, if necessary.

3. Talk with the appropriate people at your facility about room availability.

4. Start implementing your Action Plan (see below).

ACTION PLAN

My mentor's name: Karen _____

Phone: 630 779 9226 _____

Email: Karen.swanson@wheaton.edu

We ask that you complete two practicum healing groups within three months of your Initial training. These two healing groups qualify you for the Advanced level of training. Use the tables on the following pages as a guide for planning.

Group 1

	Item	What's my plan	Any action steps?
SCHEDULING	What group in your facility or on the outside will you select for your healing group?		
	When will you hold your group? (dates and time of day)		
	What schedule will you use? (i.e., 5 days in a row, 2 days one week, 3 the next, or once a week)		
PREPARING	What is classroom availability, with privacy, tables, etc.?		
	How will you recruit the class? What date?		
	Who will be leading the healing group? Co-leading?		
	Will you do any additional lessons other than the core lessons?		
	How many inmate journals will you need? Order at traumahealinginstitute.org, under "Store."		
REPORTING	When your healing group dates are fixed, email your mentor with pertinent details about your group. Consider scheduling a phone call before or during your group.		
	When you have completed your healing group, submit your healing group report* within 3 days to your mentor.		

*Download an electronic copy of the healing group report (and authorization for testimonies, if needed) from the facilitator's website (traumahealinginstitute.org/facilitators), under Reports.

Group 2

	Item	What's my plan	Any action steps?
SCHEDULING	What group in your facility or on the outside will you select for your healing group?		
	When will you hold your group? (dates and time of day)		
	What schedule will you use? (i.e., 5 days in a row, 2 days one week, 3 the next, or once a week)		
PREPARING	What is classroom availability, with privacy, tables, etc.?		
	How will you recruit the class? What date?		
	Who will be leading the healing group? Co-leading?		
	Will you do any additional lessons other than the core lessons?		
	How many inmate journals will you need? Order at traumahealinginstitute.org, under "Store."		
REPORTING	When your healing group dates are fixed, email your mentor with pertinent details about your group. Consider scheduling a phone call before or during your group.		
	When you have completed your healing group, submit your healing group report within 3 days to your mentor.		

APPENDIX

I. Recruiting Session

FACTS

Before the session begins, write these two facts on the board or flip chart:

- 97% of incarcerated women have a background of trauma
- 85% of incarcerated men have a background of trauma

At the beginning of the session, explain the facts:

- **FACT:** 97% of women who are incarcerated in the United States have a background of physical or sexual trauma and, in fact, it is their pathway to the criminal justice system.
- **FACT:** 85% of men who are incarcerated in the United States have a background of street violence trauma and 75% had sexual abuse in their background and, in fact, it is their pathway to the criminal justice system.
- **FACT:** These figures are for jails and prisons in the United States. These figures are true right here in this very facility where you are residing.

DEFINITION OF TRAUMA

Define trauma: We can be traumatized when we are overwhelmed with intense fear, helplessness, or horror in the face of death, serious injury, rape, or other forced sexual acts.

RESPONSE TO TRAUMA

Explain that people who have experienced trauma behave in three main ways: Reliving, Avoiding, Being always on alert.

Write these on the board/flip chart. Interact with inmates for the definition (e.g., "What might reliving look like?").

Ask, "Have you ever experienced any of these reactions? If so, this may indicate that you have trauma in your past that has not been resolved."

HEALING HEART WOUNDS GROUP

Say, "We will be having a Healing Heart Wounds group starting (dates/times). This group will help us work through trauma in our past. There will be five classes in all. It is a Bible-based program, but you do not have to be Christian to attend. No one will try to convert you. If you are a different religion or none at all, you can still greatly benefit from these groups."

GROUP REQUIREMENTS

- Have experienced trauma in your background and are ready to deal with it
- Do not have court or will not roll up during the class dates listed above
- No program classes scheduled during these dates
- Able to attend group meeting time

SIGN UP

"If you are interested in the class, please fill out a sign-up sheet. The class has limited space so a selection process may take place." Distribute a sign-up sheet (see next page).

HEALING HEART WOUNDS
SIGN-UP SHEET

HEALING HEART WOUNDS GROUP

We will be having a Healing Heart Wounds group starting

Date: _____

Time: _____

There will be five classes in all. It is a Bible-based program, but you do not have to be Christian to attend. No one will try to convert you. If you are a different religion or none at all, you can still greatly benefit from these groups.

GROUP REQUIREMENTS

- Have experienced trauma in your background and are ready to deal with it
- Do not have court or will not roll up during the class dates listed above
- No program classes scheduled during these dates
- Able to attend group meeting time

SIGN UP

The class has limited space so a selection process may take place.

Name: _____

Are you able to meet group requirements as listed above? Any exceptions?

_____

_____

Write why you would like to attend this group.

_____

_____

_____

_____

_____

_____

II. Healing group participation certificate

Download an electronic copy from the facilitator's website (traumahealinginstitute. org/facilitators), under Certificates.

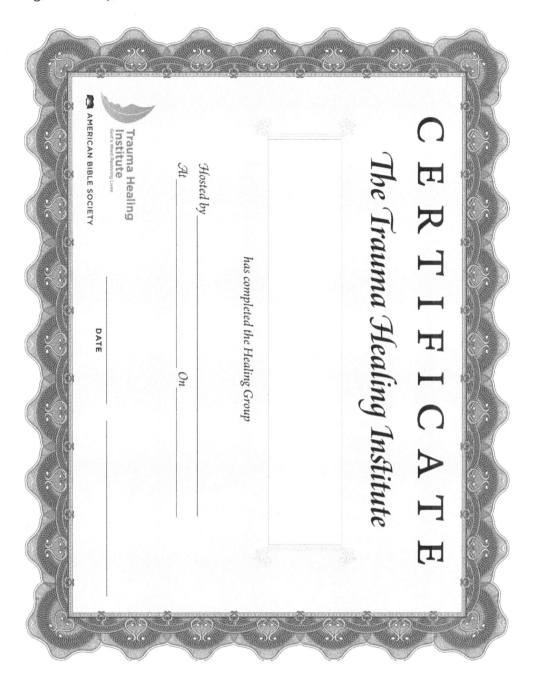

III. Healing Group Report

Download an electronic copy from the facilitator's website (traumahealinginstitute. org/facilitators), under Reports.

Location City, State, Country		Main facilitator(s)	
Host organization		Assistant facilitator(s)	
Begin date		Lessons taught	❏ ALL ❏ Core lessons ❏ 1 ❏ 2 ❏ 3 ❏ 4 ❏ 5 ❏ 6 ❏ 6A ❏ 6B ❏ 6C ❏ 7 ❏ 8 ❏ 9 ❏ 10 ❏ 11 ❏ 11A
End date			
Times and duration of meeting (1x per wk for 2 hr, all day Sat, etc.)		Number who started	
Total number of hours the class met		Number who completed	
Primary language of sessions		Number who completed who are	_____ male _____ female
Other languages used		Number of participants who completed who are	_____ Anglican _____ Catholic _____ Orthodox _____ Protestant _____ Other: _____

What successes did you experience?

What challenges did you face?

Please provide at least two testimonies, with photos and authorization if possible.

This report is available in .doc format at traumahealinginstitute.org. Send to your program administrator or to traumahealing@americanbible.org.

IV. Authorization for Testimonies & Recordings

Download an electronic copy from the facilitator's website (traumahealinginstitute.org/facilitators), under Reports.

Group authorization

Copy this page or prepare a sheet of paper with the text below and ask participants to print and sign their name to authorize use of photos and recordings that include them. Include this page with the session report.

Date:_____ Location:_____

I authorize the Bible Societies and their partners to use photos and/or voice/video recordings that include me, to promote their trauma healing programs. I'm 18 years old or older.

Name	Signature

Individual authorization

If a testimony, photo, or video can be traced to an individual, get permission before sharing. Use this form or create your own with this wording.

Description of the item: _____

I authorize the Bible Societies and their partners to use the materials in question in their ministry of promoting Trauma Healing programs. The material in question is mine and I willingly give this authorization.

Name:_____ ❏ I am 18 years old or older.

Signature:_____ ❏ Do not use my name.

Date:_____ Place:_____

V. Healing Group Checklist

Responsibilities	Details
BEFORE	
☐ Find facilitator to co-lead healing group.	
☐ Determine dates and venue of healing group.	• Identify a location based on local needs, cost, and accessibility for attendees. • Get authorization to hold healing group from appropriate leaders.
☐ Determine schedule of healing group.	• Include at least 15 min for welcome session. • Allot at least 2 hours for each lesson (combine Forgiveness lesson with "Looking Back"). • Be sure to debrief the art and lament exercises if participants do them as homework. • Do not schedule more than two lessons in one day, to protect participants from becoming overwhelmed emotionally. • Schedule snack/meal times, if applicable.
☐ If you are an apprentice facilitator, get input from your mentor about your intended schedule.	
☐ Calculate costs.	Healing groups are a part of a local ministry and should not require external funding. The only costs should be for materials, books, food, and beverages.
☐ Hold a recruiting session.	Follow suggestions in Facilitator's Guide.
☐ Purchase books.	Purchase *Healing the Wounded Heart* inmate journals.
☐ Divide the lesson sections with the co-facilitator.	Within each lesson, assign sections to different facilitators. If working with co-facilitators you haven't work with before, assign the lessons for the first sessions but wait to assign the rest until you get to know each other and who is best at what.
☐ Study and prepare for lesson sections.	Practice skits and exercises, prepare Bible references, music (if applicable).
☐ Monitor registration list.	Often, some people who register are not able to come in the end. So keep a list of additional people who would like to attend.
☐ Oversee the provision of food, drinks, and snacks, if applicable.	It is helpful to have a "host" who is responsible for this so you can focus on the lessons.
☐ Arrange for interpretation for participants, if needed.	Share the Trauma Healing materials with the translator beforehand.
☐ Prepare materials.	• Cross, if permissible • *Healing the Wounded Heart* inmate journals • Tissues • Bibles • Pens/pencils • Nametags or name tent cards • Markers/crayons • Blank paper • Flip chart, flip chart markers • Song sheets

Responsibilities	Details
☐ Remind participants of group details.	• Dates, start, and end times • Schedule • Importance of attending all sessions. Participants should speak directly with facilitator about scheduling conflicts.
☐ Meet with co-facilitator(s).	Talk through the schedule. Ensure all the lessons and sections are covered and that you have all the needed materials. Pray for the participants, the staff, and the session.
☐ Set up meeting space.	Arrange tables and chairs in a way that allows participants to interact together, ideally in a circle or at tables. Try to make it a pleasant environment.
☐ Decide who will sit at each table, if appropriate.	• Divide participants into groups of about 6 people per table. • As much as possible, make the groups diverse. • Keep the same table groups throughout the healing group.

DURING	
☐ Start with "welcome session."	See guidelines on page 7 of the *Inmate Journal*.
☐ Meet with co-facilitator at end of every day.	• Discuss learnings from day, participant concerns, and schedule modifications for next day. • If needed, talk with mentor about any concerns.
☐ Touch base with participants regularly.	Find out how they are feeling and if they are having any difficulties as a result of the healing group experience.
☐ If you are an apprentice facilitator, connect with your mentor at least once during the healing group, to talk through any questions.	
☐ Print participation certificates, if appropriate.	• Some contexts appreciate certificates, while others do not care as much. Determine if certificates would be helpful. • Download healing group participation certificate from THI facilitator's website. Fill in location, date, and each participant's name. Print and sign.
☐ If photographs are taken, ensure participants sign the Group Authorization Form.	(downloadable from THI facilitator's website)
☐ If testimonies are given, ensure participants sign the Individual Authorization Form.	(downloadable from THI facilitator's website)

AFTER	
☐ Debrief with co-facilitator.	• What were the successes? • The challenges? • What would you do differently next time? • Will any of the participants need follow up?
☐ Fill out the Healing Group report form.	• Download from THI facilitator's website or photocopy from facilitator's guide. • Fill out and email to mentor for feedback. Mentor will enter it into the Trauma Healing database or forward it to traumahealing@americanbible.org.

VI. The Inmate edition of *Healing the Wounds of Trauma*

From 2017–2019, American Bible Society consulted with Good News Jail and Prison Ministry to create *Healing the Wounded Heart: An Inmate Journal* and its accompanying facilitator's guides. These materials are adapted from *Healing the Wounds of Trauma: How the Church Can Help,* the classic Bible-based trauma healing program for adults. The contextualized materials are appropriate for use in high-security detention facilities with highly traumatized participants.

How does the inmate edition differ from the classic edition?

- The *Inmate Journal* is created for use by inmates in a healing group. Changes include adjustments in layout, design, and content.
- The stories have been revised to be more relatable to inmates.
- The activities and skits have been adapted for a secure correctional setting, where inmates are often not allowed to move around the room.
- Discussion questions have been added that allow participants to process the trauma of incarceration.
- Real stories of inmates' healing are included in each lesson.
- Relaxation exercises and coping skills are taught in each lesson to accommodate participants with high levels of trauma.
- The *Facilitator's Guide* contains all the content in the *Inmate Journal* for an easier facilitation experience.
- The *Facilitator's Guide* provides instruction on the unique aspects of leading a healing group in an incarceration setting, including getting authorization from facility leaders and recruiting participants.

List of changes between Classic edition and Inmate edition

	Classic	Inmate
Lesson 1 section 2	6 Scripture references	4 Scripture references
Lesson 1 section 4		Content moved to "Looking Back" section
Lesson 1 section 5	Includes part C (the church speaking out against evil and injustice)	Does not include part C
Lesson 1 Closing		Revisions to "Experiencing God's love" exercise
Taking care of yourself & Wrapping it up	Not included in each lesson	Included in each lesson
Lesson 2 section 2		Includes "Sources of trauma" section
Lesson 2 section 4	Water bottle activity to illustrate pushing down emotions	Index card activity to illustrate pushing down emotions
Lesson 3 section 2	Grief and trauma diagram occurs in lesson 2, section 2	Grief and trauma diagram included here
Lesson 3 section 3	Grief journey uses "Taking the journey" skit	Grief journey uses trifold paper activity or "Taking the journey" skit
Lesson 3 section 4	Includes False Bridge content	False Bridge content moved to section 3
Lesson 3 section 5	Section starts with Job example	Section starts with "What helps." Job example moved to bottom margin of facilitator's guide.

	Classic	Inmate
Lesson 8	Contains three sections	Lesson 4 in Inmate Journal Simplified to two sections by making "Share the good things God has done" an optional closing to section 2
Lesson 9		Lesson 5 in Inmate Journal
Lesson 9 section 5		Does not include "How can the church help people repent?"
Forgiveness ceremony	Included as an option	Not included. Similar content is included in "Forgiveness exercise" in Forgiveness lesson.
Looking back	Not included	Created from Classic, lesson 1, section 4 and the trauma healing experience arc included in the classic program facilitator handbook.
Initial Facilitator's Guide	Places supplemental lesson timetables in appendix	Includes new sections: • Getting authorization • Recruiting session • Next steps • Testimonies • Healing group checklist
Advanced Facilitator's Guide		Includes checklists for equipping sessions and COP events

VII. Reporting Requirements for Facilitators

Abuse of a child. If, during the course of a healing group, a facilitator learns that a minor is being sexually or physically abused, he or she must report it immediately to the proper authorities (police, child abuse hotline) and later to the church or ministry leaders, if appropriate. In many places failure to report can result in legal consequences. Reporting requirements vary, so it is important for facilitators to learn the requirements in their area (in the U.S., see childwelfare.gov for information on federal and state guidelines).

The motivation for reporting is not simply to avoid legal consequences. The protection of those who are vulnerable, especially children, is at the heart of the Christian faith (Matthew 18:6; Proverbs 31:8; Psalm 82:3-4; Deuteronomy 24:17; James 1:27). Christians are to speak up for those who are being abused and to seek justice, not just do the legal minimum. Reporting abuse against children is always the best thing for the church and for victims, even if it seems to hurt more at first.

Abuse of elders and people with disabilities. While reporting this kind of abuse to authorities is not required by law for a facilitator (in contrast to reporting child abuse), it is encouraged. (In the U.S., contact the National Adult Protective Services Association.)

Abuse of an adult. Facilitators are not required by law to report physical or sexual violence against an adult, and doing so could in fact harm the victim. Reporting must never be done without the victim's permission and should never be coerced. All decisions should be for the purpose of safety and include the victim in the planning whenever possible.

Suicide. Facilitators and people who are not mental health professionals are not required by law to report suicidal people. However, they should consider safety measures (see HWT Lesson 6B) and calling the police. (In the U.S., see the National Suicide Prevention Lifeline.)

Homicide. If a facilitator learns of a participant's intent to harm another person, the facilitator is at liberty to warn the intended victim and should strongly consider notifying the police.

CPSIA information can be obtained
at www.ICGtesting.com
Printed in the USA
FSHW020153040719
59712FS